CRISIS IN THE CURRICULUM

CRISIS IN THE CURRICULUM

EDITED BY E.C.CUFF & G.C.F. PAYNE

CROOM HELM
London • Sydney • Wolfeboro, New Hampshire

©1985 E.C. Cuff and G.C.F. Payne
Croom Helm Ltd, Provident House, Burrell Row,
Beckenham, Kent BR3 1AT

Croom Helm Australia, 44-50 Waterloo Road,
North Ryde, 2113, New South Wales

British Library Cataloguing in Publication Data

Crisis in the curriculum.
   1. Education − Curricula
   I. Cuff, E.C. II. Payne, G.C.F.
   375   LB1570

   ISBN 0-7099-3421-1

Croom Helm, 27 South Main Street,
Wolfeboro, New Hampshire 03894-2069

Library of Congress Cataloging in Publication Data

Crisis in the curriculum

   Includes index.
   1. Education − Great Britain − Curricula − Addresses,
Essays, Lectures. 2. Education − Great Britain −
Curricula − Evaluation − Addresses, Essays, Lectures.
3. Curriculum Planning − Great Britain − Addresses,
Essays, Lectures. I. Cuff, E.C. II. Payne, G.C.F.
LB1564.G7C74 1985 375'.001'0941 84-29202
ISBN 0-7099-3421-1

Reprinted 1986

Printed and bound in Great Britain by
Antony Rowe Ltd., Chippenham

CONTENTS

CONTENTS

In Memory of

GEORGE   PAYNE

1939 - 1983

We miss his drive, determination,
teaching, dry wit and, not least,
his irrepressible love of 'sport'.

Chapter One

INTRODUCTION

Ted Cuff

George Payne had the idea of producing a collection
of papers on Curriculum Issues towards the end of
1982. Quite simply, he argued that teachers,
advisers, teacher trainers, educational researchers
and others concerned with schools and what goes on
in them inevitably have views on what they see
as key issues in the school curriculum. A collection of this type would be an encouragement to
articulate these views from these various vantage
points.
    In discussing the idea of a collection of this
kind, we produced a few basic ground rules to determine what sort of contributions would be acceptable. We felt that a collection on Curriculum Issues
should be fairly eclectic, ranging across a variety
of different institutional teaching settings and a
variety of different subject areas. Some coherence
would naturally be given by the fact that all contributors were to address some aspect of the school
curriculum, but more basically, coherence would also
derive from each contribution raising issues and
pointing up conclusions of a general nature. There
would be no attempt to fit contributions into a
general scheme, grand theory or whatever dreamed up
by us as editors.
    This broad, eclectic policy was maintained in
that we were also not prescriptive on the form an
issue could take. We suggested it may be an argument for developing a new direction in a subject or
area - or even a proposal for a new subject. Or
it could question the nature of a subject. Or it
might critically examine the teaching, studying or
examining of a subject.
    What we did urge on our potential authors, how-
ever, was our preference for an approach which was
'empirical' rather than 'theoretical'. We risked

the crudity of this distinction, in order to encourage contributions which pointed to practical
possibilities and practical implications. We
felt that the best chance of such an outcome derived
from stressing the empirical relevance of contributions so that readers could most easily evaluate
the arguments in terms of recognisable and familiar
situations. Albeit, we were not concerned whether the
materials discussed derived from first hand classroom teaching or the analysis of materials derived
from observing and/or recording classroom activities,
although we anticipated that the book would include
both types of approach. By producing materials
which readers could relate to their own experiences
in schools and classrooms, we hoped to encourage
contributions with some 'authenticity'.

This notion of authenticity is in effect
epitomised in our shift from 'Curriculum Issues'
to 'Crisis in the Curriculum'. For in making our
final selection, we have ended up not only with
contributions which do have the wide and general
interest we aimed at, but they also tackle matters
of considerable concern to the respective authors.
From their standpoint the concern is more than an
'issue', it is a 'crisis'. Consequently, they feel
something - and they do suggest what - should be
be done now.

Sometimes the crisis is there for all to see.
For example, in Chapter Three Jack Hogbin and John
Bailey examine the troubles of teaching Religious
Education in the secondary school; in Chapter
Five, Ted Cuff looks at some aspects of a crisis
nationally signalled by the Cockcroft Report,
namely, teaching mathematics in both primary
and secondary schools; and in Chapter Twelve,
Tony Cassidy highlights some of the problems
involved in 'educating the educator' when he
describes his own experiences of developing staff
self-evaluation from within the school.

Sometimes the crisis becomes only too apparent
once it has been pointed out. For example, Nigel
Hall's plea for a rethinking of the teaching of
literacy skills to young children, and Digby Anderson's critical appraisal of the rhetoric which pads
out the often vacuous promise of many new curriculum
packages, may be suitable examples. Carol Cumming's
description of her experience of curriculum decision-
making in the infant school might also be included
here.

Prima facie, the other chapters may not be so
readily and easily identified as 'crisis' by some

readers, though obviously the fact of their inclusion here means that they have at least convinced us as editors. Thus George Payne and Elaine Ridge plead for teachers to enter the child's world, to appreciate their language competence and to modify their teaching methods accordingly; David Hustler and Ian Ashman sound a strong warning note on the way Personal and Social Education seems to be going; John Evans and Brian Davies argue that individuated teaching can be more rigid than some whole class approaches; Harry Osser suggests that in their use of traditional assessment procedures, teachers by and large do not really know what their pupils can do; and John Robinson and John McIntosh argue from the example of 'A' level Sociology that the examination system subverts, perhaps perverts, the nature of the subject. All of these authors suggest that if both cognisance and appropriate action is taken of their arguments, significant improvements in classroom learning can result. Viewed thus, and in these terms, these concerns do have the status of a 'crisis'.

Once the final list of contributions was decided, we could then determine their organisation in book form. We felt that a division into three sections, (a) content, (b) methods, and (c) evaluation and assessment, was a useful way of grouping them. We appreciate, however, that content, methods and assessment are features of each and every contribution. After all, the very existence of the contribution derives from the author(s) making some sort of critical assessment or evaluation of the operation of an aspect of the school curriculum; while the content and teaching methods related to this aspect of the curriculum are simply two sides of the same coin. For example, Chapter Seven on decision making in the Infant classroom has a strong bearing on content as well as raising key issues of teacher self-evaluation, but we decided it had most to say about methods. While Chapter Two on Language Development in the Infant School, or Chapter Four on Personal and Social Education could be viewed as issues of method as much as of content.

Our justifications for grouping contributions into these three sections is mainly in terms of readers' convenience. In our judgement, we have placed contributions in the most appropriate section, and the existence of these sections has enabled us to produce some introductory summaries before each of them, thereby avoiding overloading this Introduction with detailed material of this kind.

3

Instead at this point it might be more useful to
bring out the most important convergent themes
running through the various contributions.

Given the general nature of the briefing we
gave the contributors, and the range of their backgrounds and approaches, some diversity of approach,
style and presentation might be expected. Here it
should be noted that we made no attempt to iron
out these differences although we did try to
minimise the use of technical vocabulary and over-
complex syntax to ensure that meanings and intentions were as clear as possible to all interested
parties concerned with 'the curriculum'. Nevertheless, a few important themes run through the
contributions and these seem to be more than a
mere by-product of the desiderata in our briefing
to contributors.

First, most contributors stress the importance
of teachers trying to enter and understand what can
be roughly summarised as the 'child's world'. Baldly
put, there is not enough awareness of what children
can do, of what children know, whether they are in
pre-school, primary or secondary settings and
schools.

Secondly, contributors recognise that there
are no easy solutions to the problems and issues
they discuss. They are clear that the realities
of everyday life in schools make it extremely difficult for teachers to stand back and scrutinise
their own practices in order to develop and adopt
different standpoints and approaches. Consequently
contributors try to suggest practical ways forward.

Thirdly, then, insofar as the classic theory/
practice debate emerges, contributors are clear
about the need to convince the teacher-as-theorist
about what they regard as a crisis in the curriculum
It is the teacher's own theories about what is going
on in his classroom that is all-important for shaping up this practice. Generally, they refrain from
ironic comparisons from a 'detached' position.
Instead, there is emphasis on suggesting ways for
teachers to develop their own self-evaluation based
on the description and analysis of their own actual
classroom practices, what they, the teacher (and
pupils), actually do.

Finally, another major point emerges from this
emphasis on classroom practice. It concerns what
contributors take to be 'data' when fulfilling our
request that their work has 'empirical reference'.
Overwhelmingly, such data consists of reports of
observations of classroom practice, often including

transcriptions of classroom talk. There is little recourse to any kind of statistical presentation or argument. Instead, 'rich' detailed materials are preferred.

In conclusion, this book points to no less than eleven different issues concerning the school curriculum. For the respective contributors, their particular issue is a 'crisis', insofar as progress in an important area of the curriculum is checked until something is done. For those in education submerging under on-going quantitative crises concerning staffing, buildings and materials, we may seem to have mis-appropriated the word 'crisis'. Perhaps so, but we would argue as professionals in the field of education we must also address the sort of qualitative issues concerning the school curriculum that we have presented here in Crisis in the Curriculum.

SECTION   A

ISSUES OF CONTENT

This section addresses four substantive areas of the
school curriculum: early language development, the
teaching of mathematics, religious education, and personal and social education.

In their chapter, George Payne and Elaine Ridge
discount deficit models of language development for
young children. They argue that instead of faulting children in terms of what they cannot do, it is
more useful to see what they can do. Utilising the
approach of 'conversational analysis', which employs
work far less familiar than the well-known Opies
and Bernstein, they examine in some detail a transcript of at play two young children. Both are young
children, one being 7 years 11 months, the other
4 years and 5 months.

Despite this large age difference , these
authors suggest that the two children display a large
degree of interactional and conversational competence.
For in their shopping game, they show their ability
to play and to switch different roles, to move
between 'pretend' and 'real' worlds and to do so
in orderly ways. The point is that these orderly
ways depend on methodic practices available to any
adult conversationalist. For example, in adopting
rule-following behaviour, these children are not
simply following rules 'out there', laid down
by some external authority. Rather they are manifest-
ly making rules happen by employing complex interpretive skills. Such skills involve using, where
appropriate, such principles as (a) wait-and-see,
i.e. keep talking and we will see what meaning will
emerge;and (b) the etcetera principle, i.e. one can
always say more, so how much is enough for now, for
all practical purposes?

Payne and Ridge urge teachers to examine in much
more detail the talk of their young pupils as a way

of better understanding who they are, what they can
do and how they can develop. In short, they are
trying to encourage teachers to break the mould of
some prevalent though understandable practices in the
classroom treatment of young pupils, through the
understandings that can arise from trying to enter
the world of children.

In their discussion of the teaching of
mathematics and maths panic and anxiety broadly
in the age range 5-13 years, Cuff similarly urges
the importance of teachers using transcriptions
of their own lessons to examine what actually
happens in the classroom. What do their practices
look like to them? What can it be like to be a pupil
as a party in or recipient of this style of teaching?

Like language teaching nearly a decade ago,
mathematics teaching has been the subject of a major
report from a Committee of Inquiry, the Cockcroft
Report. This Report emphasises the nature of
mathematics, the importance of mathematics and the
difficulties of mathematics. Thus the subject is
hierarchically organised in conceptual terms, it can
significantly affect the world of work and everyday
life and it is extremely hard to get hold of. It is
much harder than English for example.

But why is it so hard to get hold of? Cockcroft does not strongly address this problem.
Perhaps too complacently it talks about the inherent
difficulties of Mathematics. Despite being a
'powerful, concise and unambiguous means of communication' and having 'inherently interesting and
appealing puzzles', it is difficult to get hold of
because it does not come naturally, it has to be
consciously learned, the Report says.

Although of mixed composition, the Commission
gives the feeling of mathematicians thinking and
writing about mathematics. There is a circularity
in this whole approach which gives little promise
of real development, of unblocking the 'mathematical
blockage' which has long been an observable feature
of mathematics. Somehow, the problem, what consti-
tutes this 'blockage', slips from central focus.
The nature and importance of the subject seem to
take over as the major concerns of the report.
There is discussion of maths panic and anxiety, but
it becomes just one of numerous concerns in a large
report.

As in the chapter by Payne and Ridge the
authors suggest that one problem is that not only
are mathematicians talking about mathematics, but
also adults are talking about children. Thus they

<u>know</u> what the problem is - it is to sharpen up, streamline, improve existing methods. Try harder. Change a little the mix of talk, chalk and mathematical exercises and problem solving.

For example, language is a problem in that words like 'rate', 'tessellations' have to be translated. Yet synonyms, the equivalents, the paraphrases, could be equally problematic because the translations are from a 'world of mathematics', a realm of mathematical reasoning, into an everyday world, where not only do the 'same' words (where they exist) mean something else, but they are organised differently into different <u>ways</u> of thinking about things. Moreover, this everyday world is not simply that experienced by adults. For in many ways, children can be seen to have their own culture, i.e. their own ways of organising their knowledge and their world in which adults have to be handled and dealt with.

Alternatively put, it is a passive view to see learning as the maths teacher translating the hard words and by dint of lots of patience and practice 'getting over' the subject (albeit with some speed as an organisational constraint experienced is getting through the syllabus, showing progress). This view does <u>not</u> allow for children as they are - active persons with lives of their own who make appraisals and judgements about the activities in which they are obliged to participate (e.g. mathematics).

So how <u>do</u> children experience Maths? What is 'Maths' to them? What does 'Maths' do (to them) as a label for something? What is the pupils' world like, what motivates them? What part can Maths play in the organisation of <u>their</u> world?

These questions are empirical. The answers must rely on more than attitude questionnaires and the reconstructions and retrospection of teachers, ex-teachers, and ex-pupils recalling classroom experiences. Instead, much careful, painstaking examination of actual classroom happenings has to be done.

The authors suggest that the analysis of some excerpts from transcripts of mathematics-in-action, actual classroom talk and happenings, can serve to illustrate these arguments and to point the way to making some progress towards unblocking the mathematics blockage and understanding why some children develop great anxiety, even panic, about maths. Although currently there is some excellent work being done by mathematics educators along these lines,

there seems to be little impact as yet on the
great bulk of maths lessons going on in schools
up and down the country.

If the problems of maths education seem
challenging, then the difficulties of Religious
Studies might appear overwhelming as outlined by
Jack Hogbin and John Bailey in their chapter,
appropriately entitled, 'Hard Times in Religious
Education'.

The problem of making RE a lively and viable
subject has long been familiar. Its mandatory
nature since 1944 has not resulted in an adequate
supply of curriculum time or specialist teachers
and it was flagging even before more recent pressures
such as growing secularisation, the greater ethnic
mix in schools and the growth of a new secular
competitor, Personal and Social Education.

The effect of these forces can be clearly
seen in the descriptions and analyses of the state
of the subject in three secondary schools visited
and observed by the authors. Clearly, there is no
one crisis in the place of RE in the school curriculum, but a number of interlocking crises. It is
not simply a question of resources, especially time
and specialist staff, but it is equally - or perhaps
more - a matter of purpose and direction. The
general trend of secularisation in the majority
culture and the growing presence in schools of
pupils from different minority cultures and
religions put RE as a subject under considerable
strain. So, what sort of RE is currently going on,
what sort is appropriate in this context?

The authors are in no doubt about the
'Cinderella' status of RE; a status which the three
schools examined serve to exemplify in varying degrees. Yet they feel there is hope if the practices
of one of the schools can be highlighted and developed in ways which retain the essential nature of RE.
This nature involves encouraging children to develop
a distinctive way of viewing and understanding
the world, a way that is not otherwise made available in the school curriculum. Here an alliance
with, but not a displacement by, Personal and Social
Education could be valuable, particularly in giving
RE a more practical character by way of visits and
more stimulating teaching methods. In short, PSE
must be regarded as an ally not a rival in seeking
to establish the importance of RE as a base for
critically assessing and coming to some personal
terms with society, its issues and relationships.

For David Hustler and Ian Ashman, the burning

issue in Personal and Social Education as a
curriculum subject is not primarily one of content,
but of grouping. For them, it is vital to secure a
mix of students of varying abilities and backgrounds.
This view is not argued but stated as a preference
and the chapter explores some of the politics of the
development of PSE and the likelihood of students
being taught 'apart and together'.

From their considerable experience and involvement in the field of PSE, the authors lead us through
a myriad of interrelated schemes and developments,
some old and some new, e.g. MSC, CCDU, ACS, YTS,
YMCA, TVEI, LAP, CPVE. They lead us through this
welter of acronyms to present three 'scenarios' of
possible developments in the availability of PSE.
For them, two are unacceptable: to differentiate
PSE for different types of pupils; and to abandon
PSE as a subject for the most able pupils. What they
prefer, though they are pessimistic about its chances, is the scenario of PSE as a subject for all.
A PSE of this nature in the school curriculum would
provide the basis for a social solvent in terms of
mutual understandings 'between pupils with differing
pasts and future in our society'.

They clearly believe that teachers who share
their commitment will have to fight, and fight hard,
for this scenario.

Chapter Two

"LET THEM TALK" - AN ALTERNATIVE APPROACH TO LANGUAGE DEVELOPMENT IN THE INFANT SCHOOL

George Payne and Elaine Ridge

It is current practice for most teachers to address
the business of language development in schools as
quasi-linguists, making heavy use of a deficit model.
That is to say children, especially young children
are assumed to be 'under-developed' in their use of
language and 'mistakes' or 'errors' in grammar and
expression are seen as a constant documentation of
their childlike inadequacy. The model is adopted not
through perversity on the part of teachers but
simply because it has become the established
approach peddled by academics and professionals
alike. It has been routinised as the accepted taken-
for-granted way educationalists at whatever level of
involvement in the teaching of young children
evaluate pupils' ability to use language. We wish
to propose an alternative or at least an additional
approach to the evaluation of pupils' use of language which would broaden the scope for development.
This broadening could only be beneficial because it
involves a consideration of children as culturally
worthy individuals in their own right. The culture
of childhood is an aspect of a pupil's life which is
routinely undervalued in a teacher's general judge-
mental approach to classroom performances, largely
because none of us know very much about it.
    Although the fact that children have a culture
of their own has been recognised by social scientists for quite a while now, we do not have much
knowledge of the day to day routine features of the
accomplishment of that culture.
    The studies by Iona and Peter Opie in the 1950s
and 60s give us plenty of descriptive, ethnographic
material on children's games and folklore. In their
accounts they provide a record of the language used
by schoolchildren and give us a rich description of
the content of child culture. There is, however,

little or no analysis of how this culture is organised nor of how it comes to be constructed by
children.
    More recently, sociologists with an explicit
interest in language as an element in the cultural
accomplishment of social interaction have revived
the study of children's culture. Mathew Speier is
probably the most well known. Basing his analysis
on the work of Harvey Sacks, he has argued that
whereas linguists will concentrate on linguistic
competence, that is on the ability to produce recognisable and acceptable sentences, as students of
culture we should focus our attention on 'talk'.
Talk is not just sentence production, it is the
medium through which social exchange, social co-
ordination, social interaction is accomplished.
Culture for adults and children alike is mediated,
accomplished and displayed largely through talk.
As people talk they manifest and document their
cultural assumptions and practices. Garfinkel (1967)
has argued that a noticeable feature of our world
is the presence of talk in everyday situations and
that its presence is needed if the everyday activities we get involved in are to appear normal to us.
An absence of talk on these occasions would be a
feature to be remarked upon. By studying children's
talk we would be studying their culture in operation,
studying the ways they see the world, the way they
put that world together.
    One aspect of a child's world that Speier in-
vestigates empirically is their methodical handling
of adult-child interaction. He shows that they are
able to manage that interaction in such a way that
they can make contributions to conversations despite
their vastly restricted speaking rights vis-à-vis
adults.
    One of the most recent studies of children's
culture is Bronwyn Davies', Life in the Classroom
and Playground, in which the cultural accomplishment
of school-children is set within a framework of the
child's 'double world'. Children operate in their
own world and in the world of adults. Adults on
the other hand seldom operate from within the child's
framework. In this sense the cultural achievement
of children may be seen as possibly the more
sophisticated. When children behave or talk in ways
similar to an adult they run the risk of being
viewed as 'precocious', 'cocky' or 'rude'. Children
have restricted conversational rights vis-à-vis
adults in many settings and part of being a child is
making use of the knowledge of these restricted

rights in order to behave appropriately. Although studies such as these do tell us something about the social world of childhood they only scratch the surface and do little more than identify a framework yet to be investigated. Although many classroom teachers will have heard of the Opies' work, we doubt very much that they are familiar with the works of Speier and Davies, and in that sense have not made much progress since the early 70s when Bernstein pointed to the need for teachers to know more about childhood culture. Although addressing a more limited concern, that of working class children's underachievement, at school, he displayed this awareness of the problem when he wrote, 'If the culture of the teacher is to become part of the consciousness of the child, then the culture of the child must first be in the consciousness of the teacher.'

From our own studies of children's language we can demonstrate some aspects of child culture as made available in a typical extract of children's talk. The talk was recorded in the home of one of us. There were two girls involved, one Sally aged 7 years 11 months and the other Ann is 4 years 5 months. The two children were involved in playing a 'pretend' game of 'shop'. They had organised the game entirely on their own, with no suggestions, directions or interventions from any adult.

We will set the scene in a little detail to enable the reader to put the talk as represented in the transcription into an appropriate context.

A downstairs room in the house was used as the 'shop' (no other children or adults were present in this room at the time). Various objects had been set out on a table, to represent goods for sale, by Sally (7:11). This had taken about 4-5 minutes. In the meantime Ann (4:5) had been excluded from the room and had gone upstairs to get her doll and pram in anticipation of her forthcoming already designated role as 'customer'. Ann can be heard in the earlier part of the transcript to be singing and talking to her doll. She had also called out (using Sally's real name) to ask if the shop was open yet and had been told 'it's still night-time' and later on, when she asked a second time, was told 'it's nearly morning'. Sally had then come out of the room, changed the 'closed' sign on the door to 'open' and gone back into the room, shutting the door behind her. Ann was heard to remark 'Open -- I can go in now' and could be heard coming down the stairs with the pram, still singing and talking to

13

the 'baby'. Also a point to note is that the children are, in the subsequent transcript, not using their normal everyday speaking voices, rather, using 'stage' voices.

The extract of talk begins at the point where the game 'proper' begins, the previous activities being reasonably seen as the preliminary preparation for it, during which appropriate roles had been assigned or 'mapped' onto the respective children. Sally being the shopkeeper and Ann being the customer. At this point it is suggested that the transcript of the talk is read.

Transcription of the children's talk

	Ann	((5 knocks at the door))
1.	Sally	Come i:n
2.	Ann	He:llo
3.	Sally	D-yer-know-what
4.	Ann	What
		((Pause circa 3 seconds))
5.	Sally	You can ha:ve - something free
6.	Ann	What we don't have to pay
7.	Sally	Yes - you can have one thing free
8.	Ann	Oh - thank you
9.	Sally	Pick it na
10.	Ann	Whoops-a-daisy ---- I was want, - this - this stand this is one thing cos it goes togevver doesn't it// ((The stand is a doll's carry cot stand, and the carry cot goes with it))
11.	Sally	( ) yeh - now you don't have to pay for it
12.	Ann	Thank you -- darling -- would you be quiet I've just brought you a new stand you kno:w - - - don't want you saying it doesn't - you don't like it - - else you'll get a smack//( )
13.	Sally	Ah she will because it's very comfortable you know
14.	Ann	Thank you - - thank-you-very-much ((sing song voice)) - - darling and I must never say that again you're always very cheeky ((pause circa 2 seconds)) ((singing)) If you like - - have you got a baby
15.	Sally	Me
16.	Ann	Yes
17.	Sally	Have I got-a-baby
18.	Ann	Yes

19.	Sally	No - - I don't like babies yer-see ((said quietly))
20.	Ann	Have you got children
21.	Sally	No -- yes -- I-have-<u>one</u>// but they've left home
22.	Ann	How old is it -- what
23.	Sally	They're - - they are nineteen ((Pause circa 3 seconds))
24.	Ann	Oh where are they
25.	Sally	They're in -- e:r - Debby
26.	Ann	Oh where-do-you-live
27.	Sally	In Southam
28.	Ann	O:h they <u>must</u> have got married
29.	Sally	Yes they have - - - I went to their wedding ((Pause circa 4 seconds))
30.	Ann	Oh dear dear (I'm) gonna invite them to my baby's party cos it's tomorrow
31.	Sally	They'll be able to come -- I'll ask them
32.	Ann	Er - just a minute// ( )
33.	Sally	They <u>love</u> babies yer know -- they already have one themselves
34.	Ann	Er can the <u>baby</u> come then - (you'll) pretend you're a baby then OK ((last part of utterance said in a soft voice))
35.	Sally	No I'm-not-a-baby (I can't)
36.	Ann	Well <u>you</u> could be the <u>helper</u> with me
37.	Sally	I ( ) can't cos I have to open the shop ((last part of utterance spoken quietly))
38.	Ann	Well -- doncha-know
39.	Sally	(What)
40.	Ann	its someone's wedding as <u>well</u>
41.	Sally	I know I love weddings but <u>I</u> just can't go to them
42.	Ann	( )
43.	Sally	See the shop's closing down
44.	Ann	What
45.	Sally	The shop's closing now
46.	Ann	Well -- do-you-know you could sleep
47.	Sally	I wish I could -- I'll sleep some other day when I've done my work
48.	Ann	OK e:r we'll do some decorations for when you come OK
49.	Sally	O(hh)K thanks very much

50. Ann   By:e baby no cheeky you get cheeki-
            ness --- please --- cos you're going-
            to-have-a a very happy day in a few
            days time ((Pause circa 7 seconds and
            sounds of the pram being dragged
            upstairs)) Darling and now don't --
            be any nonsense at all (   ) you're
            a nonsense person you know a
            very nonsense...
            ((tape untranscribable as voice be-
            came indistinct as Ann continues up
            the stairs)).

In approaching this talk as a display of children's
culture in operation, we make the assumption, follow-
ine Sacks, that interactants, through engaging in
practical activities together, routinely deal with
interactional 'problems', the solutions to which
can be found in the organisation of their talk. It
is through this general procedure that interactions
can be accomplished relatively smoothly. In this
talk the children can be heard to be relating to a
number of potential problems and though their competence at providing solutions to them accomplish
the interaction required to make the game. In providing for the solutions in their talk they are displaying skilful use of methodic practices and un-
doubted interactional competence in language use.
We shall attempt to describe that competence.
     Generally, the children display through their
talk a main concern to 'keep the game going' which
involves them making decisions about applying rules
relating to pretend games and managing an acceptable
tolerance of any circumstances or mistakes that arise.
Problems of this nature are to be found in all games
but on any occasion the decisions will be 'context
specific' that is, will be relevant to that particular
occasion. In this occasion represented we suggest
that the children can be heard to be orientating
to at least three potential problems that arise out
of their consideration of three features of this
situation. These features assume importance in this
situation, i.e. they are orientated to as relevant
features to be taken into account whilst engaging in
the interaction of the game. They are not necessarily to be found as typical features of most standard
games of shop, although we suspect one or more of
them are quite likely to occur in other games.
     The first feature is the age difference. There
is some three and a half years between the players.
This difference could pose potential problems in

relation to their different experience and knowledge
of real shops, playing pretend games and conversational skills of the two children Sally is likely to
have greater experience in these areas, which may provide her with a taken-for-granted higher status than
Ann and consequently to give Sally certain potential
'rights'.

The second feature is the <u>physical arrangement</u>
of the setting itself. The setting up of the shop
in an enclosed room means that the 'customer' is
excluded from the main setting when she is not actively engaged in the business of buying something.
Often "shops' may be set up in a corner of a room
or outside, where customers and the shopkeeper have
opportunities to remain in visual and aural contact
and monitor each others activities.

The third feature is the <u>presence of only 2
players</u>, this being the minimum necessary in order
for the game to proceed. Although a game of shop
may be enlarged to include delivery men, window
cleaners, policemen etc the minimum requirement
for a full complement of players is one shopkeeper
and one customer. Setting up the game in the way
they have, these children display their knowledge
and recognition of the minimum number of categories
in this game set. Their use of the categories
shopkeeper and customer shows their cultural knowledge of how these 'standardised relationship pairs[1]
work in this setting. These more context specific
problems, however, are oriented to within a broader
framework of relevance of playing pretend games.

As Sacks (1965) has indicated in playing pretend
games, one overriding problem which actors orient to is
the legal/illegal rule. He says that in pretend games
where play consists of simulating the actions of
some <u>possible</u> real environment, and necessarily rests
on the principle that pretend facts must be able to
be treated as if they were real facts, the following
rule operates: an action is legal if it is deemed
possible in the real environment, and it is illegal
if the players decide it is not possible. Therefore,
actions in play environments get treated by references to real environments. In children's games
illegal actions 'don't count' as part of the game,
they are invalid as far as the game is concerned.
One can expect in pretend games that certain actions
may become the cause of a dispute, the legality or
otherwise of the actions may be solved by discussion
and relate to different children's knowledge of the
real world. In the interactional situation under
consideration potential problems concerning the

17

legality or otherwise of certain actions could
possibly be accentuated by the presumed relative
lack of experience of the younger child vis-à-vis
the older one, and this could affect their individual perceptions of rule violations and the subsequent treatment of them. The absence of any
third party to help in the settlement of disputes
means that it is likely to be a one-against-one
conflict. The solution the girls use is one routinely used by adults i.e. in the interests of getting on with various practical projects when one
interactant is presumed by both not to be as know-
ledgeable as the other, the solution is simply to
relax the rules. Thus where potential conflict or
disagreement and ambiguities arise, interactants
can make use of an overriding rule which could be
stated: if the action or utterance which is potentially disputable, is not too important or disruptive, let it pass. This rule is used by both
the member adjudged more competent and the less competent member. Sally in relation to this rule, can
also use in addition, the cultural maxim 'make allowances for children younger than yourself' as a resource in the interests of keeping the game going.
    We suggest that a general strategy a teacher
can use to try to gain an insight into the culture
of the child is to resist the temptation to make
simplistic judgements about pupils. To become aware
of the features of a situation oriented to by children which is made available in their talk is to come
closer to an understanding of aspects of their culture. In turn, that understanding can help to avoid
making simplistic judgements about children.
    For example, should a teacher notice that a
child is having some 'difficulty' in class it is
most likely to be beneficial to try to discover
which features of the particular context in question
are significant for that child. By attempting to
get inside the child's frame of reference, the
teacher would be in a better position to help the
child overcome its difficulties. The more usual
orientation in teaching involves an attempt to get
the child to move into the teacher's frame of reference (see for example Mary Willes, 1981), Cicourel
et al (1974), forcibly argue this point in their description of how children use language at home and at
school. They suggest that in order to attempt an
adequate understanding of children's responses, particularly in the 'test' situation, we must try to understand the reasoning processes that led to them and

consequently find out which features of the context are being oriented to by the children as relevant features of the task. Cicourel and his colleagues were specifically investigating testing situations and their studies revealed that 'right answers' can arise from many different reasoning processes and strategies adopted by the children in different settings, some of which could be considered as incorrect in relation to the particular skill being tested.   Conversely, they found that children can arrive at 'wrong answers' though using the correct reasoning process because they also attend to part- icular features of the context which the test con- structors and the teachers had not supposed they would take into account. The production of 'right' and 'wrong' answers are not automatically indicative of correct or incorrect reasoning processes, they are the product of orienting to selected significant features of a situation. What children orient to will to some extent be influenced by their cultural perceptions and priorities. Knowing more about children's culture will certainly benefically effect a teacher's evaluation of what they can do.

Our own analysis of the young children's talk reinforces this view in that it indicates how child- ren are not always attending simply to what adults take to be the obvious relevant features of a con- text. If for example we judged Sally and Ann's per- formance and talk simply with reference to the sim- ilarity it bore to the 'real' world, their perform- ance could be judged imperfect and full of mistakes. Whereas by attempting to recognise the many concerns to which they were attending and providing solutions for, their performance can be viewed in a new light and be seen as thoroughly competent. In our extract of talk there are a number of topical ambiguities and contraditions which might be considered on a first reading to be the kinds of mistakes and am- biguities which are normal features of most con- versations between competent adults. Alternatively, however, they may also be generated out of the spec- ific difficulties experienced by children in the playing of pretend games. A noticeable feature in pretend games is that the facts about <u>oneself</u> are pretend facts. Thus interactants have to remember not only the pretend facts that they are hearing about the other person (which usually conflict with the real known facts about that person), but sim- ultaneously have to construct and remember facts about their newly emerging 'pretend self'. Any adult who has ever, in 'role games' for example, pretended

to be someone else, or even simply fabricated a few
'pretend facts' about what they have done, will
readily appreciate the extra difficulty it imposes
in relation to one's memory and concentration in
trying to incorporate these facts and sustain their
credibility in ordinary conversation. We suggest
that children who regularly play pretend games are
aware of these difficulties, they orient to them
as part of their commonsense knowledge about pretend
games, and tend to make allowances for them by in-
voking the afore-mentioned rules.

It would certainly seem to be the case that the
interactional episode represented by the children's
talk is very complex and requires a not inconsider-
able degree of conversational competence from those
participating in it. We assume that children's
background knowledge and experience provides them
with resources for generating appropriate talk and
activities in particular contexts. In this case
the children's commonsense knowledge and experience
of what is involved in playing pretend games and
their generalised knowledge of social life are used
as resources for organising their talk appropriately
in this occasion.   The appropriateness of the
talk makes available to us the conversational competence of the children. We can examine that competence more closely, considering one of the 'mistakes' which might lead adults to assume some inadequacy or impoverishment in language use.

At the beginning of the extract we can hear:

> Ann   ((5 knocks at the door))
> Sally   Come i:n

Certainly one could argue that this is not the
usual way a person enters a shop, and therefore
it could be taken as evidence of both children's
imperfect view of reality and an inappropriate
thing to say. Further our acquaintance with the
children and our knowledge that they do not knock
on doors before entering shops might easily lead us
to a judgement of incompetence.

However, looked at in other ways this beginning is quite appropriate and displays a considerable interactional competence in this situation.
It is accepted by both children, i.e. it is not
challenged with reference to the legal/illegal
rule on the grounds that both girls recognise that
Sally is the leader.   This knowledge can be seen
to be demonstrated in later stages of the talk, but
suffice it to say at this point that Ann's

knowledge and acceptance of Sally's leader status
has been displayed in her initial acceptance of
her own non-lead role, i.e. the 'customer', in the
game, and is also shown in the pre-game talk where
Ann can be heard to wait upstairs until Sally is
ready to begin the game. She twice asks if the shop
is open, and does not come down until she sees Sally
change over the sign on the door.   She has not at
this stage, however, had verbal confirmation that
Sally is ready to begin and she needs this a) because although she knows the sign has been changed
it is likely that she is not yet able to read that
it does in fact say 'open', and b) she has no way of
seeing into the shop to confirm that the game has
indeed started, as the door has no windows in it.
By knocking on the door she is in fact asking Sally
to confirm, as the leader of the game, that the game
has indeed started. Sally's reply 'come i:n' can
be taken as confirmation that the game has started
and also of Sally's leadership as one who has the
right to decide this.   By making use of the overriding rule in the interests of getting the game
started, and possibly Sally's use of the maxim 'make
allowances for little children', they also confirm
the status of Ann and Sally relative to each other.
Thus knocking at the door can be seen to be an
acceptable albeit illegal way of starting the game
bearing in mind the variety of features that the
children are orienting to.
      When viewed in these terms the utterances can
be seen to represent sophisticated interactional
skills and appropriate use of language.
      Moving to another section of the talk we can
see further evidence of sophisticated language
competence in dealing with ambiguities and conf-
usions which could result in a potential breakdown
in understanding between the two girls.

20.	Ann	Have you got children
21.	Sally	No--Yes---I-have-<u>one</u> but they've left home
22.	Ann	How old is it--what
23.	Sally	They're - - they are nineteen ((Pause circa 3 seconds))
24.	Ann	Oh where are they
25.	Sally	They're in--e:r:Debby
26.	Ann	Oh where do you live
27.	Sally	In Southam ·
28.	Ann	O:h they must have got married then
29.	Sally	Yes they have---I went to their wedding

		((Pause circa 4 seconds))
30.	Ann	Oh dear dear (I'm) gonna invite them to my baby's party cos its tomorrow
31.	Sally	They'll be able to come--I'll ask them
32.	Ann	Er--just a minute//( )
33.	Sally	They <u>love</u> babies yer know --they already have one themselves
34.	Ann	Er can the <u>baby</u> come then - (you'll) pretend you're a baby then OK

It is noticeable that although Ann does not seek
clarification of who 'they' are, and thereby receives
none from Sally, the two girls continue the conversation and manage, by utterance 29 to construct together an acceptable understanding of whom the pronoun
represents. 'They' now refers to a married couple, one
of which is the shopkeeper's son or daughter. Possibly the girls did not bother to seek clarification
of the meaning of 'they' earlier, because they were
waiting to see how it would turn out, or because of
their knowledge of the nature of facts in pretend
games, for it must happen quite often in pretend games
where players are building up the situation as they
go along, that a player herself is not quite sure
about what she's doing or may even forget. However,
this does not matter as long as between them, they
manage to construct some acceptable i.e. 'legal'
elements.   Pretend facts are recognised as being
being qualitatively different to real facts, they are
less stable and do not directly relate to persons and
activities in the way 'real' or 'true' facts do.
Thus one might not yet know what the 'pretend facts'
are going to be, or one might decide to change them.
Pretend facts are therefore more tentative and pro-
visional than real ones.   This knowledge of the
nature of pretend facts allows both children to let
utterance 21 pass as appropriate and without comment.
In an ordinary conversation an answer 'No--Yes'
to a question 'Have you got children?' would be
noticeable as strange, and thought to be either a
slip of the tongue, or, considering the pause between
No and Yes, more likely to be heard as an attempt
to conceal the information followed by a decision
not to do so.   In a pretend game however this can be
interpreted as someone having 'changed their mind'.
Similarly in utterance 21 'I have one//but they've
left home' can be interpreted as Sally having changed
her mind and now having more than one child.   Following utterance 23 'They're-- they are nineteen' might
lead us, as adults, to make the assumption that

'they' are probably twins, but this interpretation is probably one that is not immediately
available to Ann because of her inexperience in this
area although it may have been Sally's intention to
pretend she had twins. Ann continues with her
questioning and ascertains that 'they' live in a
different town to their mother and draws on her
cultural understanding as to what that might mean,
suggesting - "Oh they must have got married then'.
This would be a reasonable assumption for her to
make. Older children living in a different town
from their mothers in her experience are usually
married, that is the reason for them moving away.
The 'they' at this point could still in fact be the
shopkeeper's two children who are living in the same
town. In utterance Sally says 'Yes they have--I
went to their wedding". By the use of the word
wedding, she has effectively constituted 'they'
as a couple, one of which (referring back retrospectively to the one in utterance 21) is her grown
up child. By utterance 33, 'They love babies you
know--they already have one themselves" the 'they'
can be understood to be unambiguously referring once
again to a married couple. Thus an appropriate
understanding of 'they' has been jointly achieved
by utterance 29 and this meaning sustained and confirmed in utterance 33.
   Our brief analysis demonstrates some of the
conversational/interaction skills these children
are displaying in their talk as they orient to the
features of the situation significant for them. For
example, we can note that they are making use of the
interpretive procedures discussed by Cicourel and of
some invariant conversational rules described by
Sacks et al. Both children in finding an appropriate
sense in the utterances we have just been examining,
20-34, can be heard to be making a retrospective -
prospective analysis of the conversation, employing
the wait-and-see principle in order to decide the
possible meaning of the present utterance and of what
was said before. Additionally they make use of the
et cetera assumption, assuming that others will 'fill
in' their intended meaning and thus display their
tacit reliance of members' common understandings.
   For example, Ann in utterance (24) 'Oh where
are they' makes use of a normal form of expression
that is potentially ambiguous i.e. it could have
been answered in a variety of ways such as e.g. in
bed, in England, in an aeroplane etc. Here it can
be recognised as a deliberate and strategic 'search
procedure' to help her to decide what kind of

children, children who are 19, are. We would suggest that her understanding of what a child of nineteen is like, is slight. Sally chose to make sense of the expression by hearing it as 'where do they live'. This is an appropriate sense for the utterance in this context and is accepted as such by Ann who in turn displays her understanding of Sally's utterance through her response and further to tying in her next question; 'Oh where do you live?' to the previous two utterances. Another point in the interaction where Ann has to accomplish what appears to be strong repair work is when she has tried to find a suitable sense for 'Debby'. It may be that Debby possibly has a kernel meaning for Ann as a girl's name, but it could well be the first time that she had encountered the word. Yet she managed to make sense of it by correctly understanding it to be a possible town, possibly through a retrospective analysis of her own question in utterance 24 and Sally's answer in utterance 25. She does in fact in utterance 26 consequently display her understanding of Debby as a town by using the less ambiguous utterance 'Where do you live' to preserve continuity.

In addition, through the perseverance displayed in their continuing to converse with each other even in the course of this apparently confused exchange they can be seen to be orienting to a reciprocity of perspectives. That they continue with the conversation indicates an assumption that they will eventually understand what each other means because they live in essentially the same world. We can see their use of their common sense reasoning, cultural understandings and methodic practices as they make sense of the sequence of utterances and thereby accomplish the interaction of the occasion through their conversational competence.

This conversational competence is also made available through their observable knowledge of the technical features of two party conversations. Thus Ann's knowledge of the implications of the use of a summons, i.e. that typically it receives an answer and Sally's knowledge of an appropriate answer was a resource used by the girls to begin the game. As Schegloff suggests, it is a most powerful way of governing conversational interaction. Through Ann's knocking and Sally's response the game is quickly set in motion. We can also note the use of 'er', 'well', 'oh' and 'ah' as carefully selected pre-entry devices used to secure the next turn. The children's talk also displays the usual 2 party pattern of turn

24

taking ABABAB - -. They have managed to slot in
their utterances, with only a few instances of over-
lapping (and these have been dealt with in methodic
ways).

Concerning topicality, most utterances display
fairly obvious topical relevance to those that have
gone before. In two places, the end of utterance
14, and utterance 46 & 47 the topical continuity
could be doubted by naive hearers. The last part
of Ann's utterance in utterance 14 could be heard
as having no topical connection to her previous
conversation with the shopkeeper i.e. the utterance
'If you like -- have you got a baby'. However, it
can be considered topically relevant through the
methodical way she uses it to link two separate
conversations (i.e. that of the shopkeeper and
customer, and that of the baby and customer).
Through thereby redefining the conversation as a
3-party one, she is enabled to re-open her conversation with the shopkeeper and at the same time
change the topic whilst retaining topical continuity.
Thus, having been scolding the baby within the shopkeeper's hearing, it is quite legitimate that she
might enquire whether she too had a baby. To do
this also involved the re-categorisation of the shopkeeper as a 'possible mother' and consequently
changing the context within which to interpret the
talk, and to change the relationship between the
shopkeeper and customer to one that takes account
of the relationship that might exist between mother
talking to another mother as well. The two girls
are now relating to each other as 'customer and
mother' talking to 'shopkeeper and mother'. For
conversations involving more than 2 persons, separate
conversations often start up between different participants and may join together again, using methods
of this nature.

In utterance 47, we can see that Sally manages
to handle the potentially ambiguous preceeding
utterance of Ann (Utterance 46) 'Well--do-you-know-
you could sleep' which would seem to have little
or no connection with any previous part of the conversation. We suggest her answer 'I wish I could - -
I'll sleep some other day when I've done my work' can
be heard to indicate her retrospective analysis of
the conversation which took place prior to the
official beginning of the game, and ties back to two
of her own utterances made at that time. While she
was setting up the shop, she delayed Ann's entrance
by saying firstly that it was 'night time' and
later that it was 'nearly morning'. We suggest that

she interpreted Ann's comment 'you could sleep' to
refer back to these utterances, and her subsequent
understanding that Ann might have interpreted these
to mean that Sally as a shopkeeper, had been working
all through the night, and consequently might be
tired.

From this conversation we can see that children
are using sophisticated methodic practices to
begin and sustain this conversation and episode
of interaction. Our recognition of that competence
comes in part from an attempt to get inside the
cultural resources they call upon as reasonable
competent interactional members of society and
especially as children.

The main thrust of our proposal, following
Speier's line of argument, is that teachers should
make more use of the practical possibility for
finding out more about children's culture by studying
the language they used to talk. This study could be
facilitated by making 'talk development' as distinct
from language development, an integral part of the
curriculum. Talk is the major medium through which
social life operates. Leiter (1981) has commented
recently that for many activities talk itself is
the main involvement and suggest that it is probably
the reason why often the main criterion on which we
base our judgements about people's competence in
routine situations is their competence in talk
production, that is their ability to talk sensibly.

Similarly in classrooms, especially infant
classrooms, judgements are made about children
largely on the evidence of what they say.   The
point we wish to make most strongly is that in order
to make judgements about a child's performance and
ability or lack of ability, as displayed in their use
of language, some effort should be made to take into
account the nature of that language use as talk and
the nature of the social world from in which it is
produced. To make judgements with reference only to
the features of the social world which are obvious to
the teacher runs the risk of misunderstanding the
significance of the pupils' talk and behaviour and
consequently making erroneous inferences about the
child's capabilities and difficulties. Making 'talk
development' an integral part of the curriculum would
not only have the aim of improving the child's talking ability, it would also provide an opportunity
for teachers to study child culture whilst actually
teaching.

As they come to know more about the nature of
childhood so closer relationships between pupils and

the curriculum can be forged.   The obvious advantages of any such moves would include increased meaningfulness for pupils.   Pupils would see a relevance to themselves in their studies and that would in turn decrease the possibilities for feelings of alienation.

In their approach to 'talk development', however, it is most important that teachers recognise the high degree of competence enjoyed by even the youngest of children.   It is clear from our own analysis and from the work of Sacks and Speier in particular that children are much more interactionally competent than they are usually given credit for.   They are more skilful in talking than many teachers realise because attention is more usually focused on language development rather than talk.

To produce any conversation is indeed a sophisticated skill.   In any conversation people do not know precisely what they are going to say to each other.   What one says in each turn is usually dependent on what the other person(s) says, and one can never know for sure exactly what that will be until it has been said.   (That is not to say that we do not decide in advance what we would like to say and make reasonable guesses as to what other people might say).   Not knowing what others are going to say and for how long they are going to speak would seem to pose potential problems, and yet children routinely carry on conversations with apparent ease including the routine handling of apparent mistakes when they occur.

In our analysis we have demonstrated some of the social competence involved in producing sensible talk and conversation.   We can expand on that a little more now by referring to the broad interpretative procedures Cicourel has suggested are the prerequisites to any member's ability to produce sensible talk through their knowledge of social structure and the way it works.

Cicourel (1967) identifies these interpretative procedures as (a) the <u>reciprocity of perspectives</u>, which operates on the assumption that if one member were to change places with another, each would see the world from the other's perspective, small differences due to their unique biographies could be ignored 'until further notice';   (b) the use of <u>normal forms</u>, a procedure through which each member assumed that they or 'anybody' else can produce normal forms of both talk and appearances, that 'anyone' can understand, thus sustaining a sense

of the world as it is.   Through this procedure
members can perceive facts and such things as
typicality, likelihood, comparability, causal
texture and means-ends relationships;   (c) the
etcetera procedure which enables members to 'fill
in' intended meanings and tacit knowledge;   (d)
the 'wait and see procedure' which Cicourel calls
'the retrospective-prospective sense of occurrence'.
It is through the use of this procedure that members,
if they have difficulty in making sense of an utterance, can assume that the speaker will say something
later that, through a retrospective-prospective
analysis of the conversation, will allow them to fill
in 'the meaning', or it may be that the sense of the
previous utterance will be revised;   and (e) the
procedure which assumes that descriptive vocabularies
are indexical expressions.   This means that in order
to decide the sense of a particular utterance, we
need to go beyond the kernal meaning of the individual words and link them to the context, which
includes noting who the speaker is, his purpose,
the setting, his relationship with the hearer and
other relevant features of the particular occasion.
     In addition to these interpretative procedures,
competent talkers also make use of invariant rules
of conversational construction.   Sacks and his
associates have described how these rules are routinely used to begin and end conversations, and to
sustain the talk in between through practices such
as attending to topicality and taking turns
appropriately.
     This range of competences is involved in the
production of routine conversations and children
appear to acquire them very early in their lives.
How they acquire them is still a mystery as yet to
be discovered, although Sacks' (1965) analysis of
children's games leads him to suggest that games
might provide children with a potent setting where
much of this learning can take place.   With regard
to the infant school curriculum, we are suggesting
that games are aspects of children's language
competence of which teachers are largely ignorant.
But there is no good practical reason for them to
continue to remain so.
     Teachers could approach the matter system-
atically by providing opportunities for 'talk time',
and 'games time' as they do now, but perhaps engage
in them more actively by trying to see the world as
their pupils see it.
     Through attempting to enter into what Schutz
has called a we-relationship with their pupils, they

28

can make efforts to see the world as children do.
Bronwyn Davies has described how entering a we-
relationship with the pupils she studied, that is a
relationship in which she tried to see the world
as they saw it whilst getting them to see the world
as she saw it, she was able to discover aspects of
children's culture hitherto unknown to her and to
come to understand their talk differently.

At the same time, however, it is most important that some attempt is made to monitor talk by
tape-recording and possibly videoing it. Some
infant schools organise their days so that one half,
usually the morning, is spent doing maths or number
work and writing and in the other half, the afternoon, the children get a 'free choice' when they
might do some craft or 'play'. In this 'free choice'
period all the talk that is produced is generally
left unmonitored, unrecorded and unexplored in
detail. It should not be difficult to capture some
of this freely available talk on tape. Ancillary
helpers or visiting mothers, not uncommon in infant
schools, could be a tremendous help in this
endeavour.

Then having captured the talk it can be analysed for the competence it displays, for the interactional and social knowledge and development it
shows or does not show and for how it relates to
teacher perceptions of the pupils.

In time the analysis might come to concentrate
on the children's use of the interpretative procedures and on the invariant rules of conversation
production in fine detail, but to begin with we
suggest that teachers could focus on two broad
aspects at a lower level of analytical rigour.
They could consider (a) how a child understands
and produces understandable utterances in conversations or talk through the use of methods of
common sense practical reasoning and (b) how the
child constructs a conversation in a technical
sense, that is by speaking at appropriate times,
about appropriate topics and so on. To some
extent these two aspects interrelate, but it might
be useful to start off with this distinction and to
see how the interrelations arise. In that way the
interrelationship between the organisation of the
talk and world views of the children might become
more apparent. We believe we have provided some
idea of the flavour of the kind of analysis which is
possible in our own attempt to delve into the talk
of Ann and Sally.

In principle there is no reason why 'talk

development' and the simultaneous study of it and
child culture should be restricted to the infant
school curriculum. It could well continue into the
junior and the secondary school. At the secondary
school level there would appear to be links between
the notions of interactional language competence and
'life and social skills'. Perhaps some children on
leaving school find themselves disadvantaged in the
world because of a lack of conversational competence.
It may be that there is a place for the development
of talking skills in all levels of education. We
certainly believe there is a place for it in infant
schools where conversational skills are developing.
The irony is that young children have already developed at that stage of their life much more competence than most teachers recognise and the question
of developing it further is seldom contemplated.

Finally, to place our proposal in a wider context of curriculum evaluation and development we
would point out that the 'talk development' is just
one possibility. It represents one attempt to move
teachers out of an apparently institutionalised
ignorance of conversation.

The fact of the matter is that most teaching is
blind; it is an act of faith.   Teachers present
ideas and knowledge to their pupils with a minimal
awareness of how such things are processed and
understood by the recipients. Although to the teaching profession these may sound heretical statements,
we would argue that it does not take much consideration to recognise that they are observably true.

How many teachers really know how language
is processed by the brain, know how talk and actions
relate to thoughts and the operation of the human
mind.   No one really seems to know.   It only takes
a brief survey of the literature in this field of
study to realise there is a wide diversity of viewpoints and an almost total lack of established empirical evidence on the matter.   It may be claimed
from time to time that we can know the minds of people
really close to us, but if we think about even that
possibility in detail, it is an extremely doubtful
claim.

If this seemingly inevitable ignorance is true
for two people who have a very close relationship.
consider how it must be in the nature of the situation for teachers and pupils in a classroom.   The
very characteristics of the classroom situation
exacerbate the ignorance.   A one-to-one social
situation in a classroom, where the teacher may be
dealing with thirty or so children, can only be

fleetingly experienced. More pertinently, the press
of the immediate occasion requires a teacher to act,
to cope, to manage things in a manner which denies
even the opportunity to consider the issue of what
might really be going on inside the pupil's head.
The features of the classroom situation appear to
force teachers to do things that they know in their
heart of hearts are inadequate.   Unfortunately
this perceived impotence in the teacher's lot seems
to generate an unchallenged conservatism in matters
of the curriculum, particularly with regard to
young pupils.   They tend to take the subjects in
the curriculum for granted.
    The range of abilities and skills which young
children possess when they enter school is very
selectively addressed by the current curriculum.
Clearly some selection is inevitable because teachers
cannot do everything, but our concern is that the
selection tends to become ossified into 'the usual'
pattern and thereby large areas of potential do not
get developed. This underdevelopment is not so
much intentional as an unnoticed consequence of
the lack of awareness by teachers of their ignorance
about children, coupled with the fact that contin-
uously they have to cope with the practical press
of the social situation of the classroom.

NOTES

    1.   'Standardised relationship pairs' in our
culture are certain categories which we routinely
recognise as paired categories, e.g. husband and
wife, mother and child and, as in this case, shopkeeper and customer. The pairing is recognised as
incorporating standardised relationships of rights,
obligations and expectations. For fuller explan-
ation see H. Sacks, 'The search for help: no-one
to turn to' in E.S. Schneidman (ed) <u>Essays in Self
Destruction</u> (Science House) 1967.

REFERENCES

Bernstein, B. 'Education cannot compensate for
        society' p.65 in Cosin et al, op. cit.
Cicourel, A.V. <u>Language Use and School Performance</u>,
        Academic Press Inc. 1974.
Cicourel, A.V. 'The Acquisition of Language Social
        Structure: Towards a Developmental Sociology
        of Language of Meaning', in Douglas, J.D.
        (eds) <u>Understanding Everyday Life</u>, Routledge
        and Kegan Paul, 1971.

                                              31

Davies, B. Life in the Classroom and Playground
    Routledge and Kegan Paul, 1982.
Garfinkel, H. Studies in Ethnomethodology, Prentice
    Hall Inc., 1967
Leiter, K. A Primer on Ethnomethodology, Oxford
    University Press, 1981
Sacks, H. 'On some formal properties of children's
    games' pre-draft 2, Unpublished mimeo, 1965
Sacks, H. 'On the analyzability of stories by child-
    ren' in Turner, Roy (ed) Ethnomethodology,
    Penguin, 1974.
Schegloff, E. 'Sequencing in conversational openings'
    in Laver, J. & Hutchinson, S. (eds) "Communica-
    tion in Face-to-face Interaction", Penguin 1973.
Speier, M. How to observe face-to-face communication:
    A Sociological introduction, Goodyear, 1983 also
    'The child as a conversationalist: some culture
    contact features of conversations between adults
    and children', in Cosin et al School and Societ
    Routledge and Kegan Paul, 1971
Willes, M.'Children becoming pupils: a study of
    discourse in nursery and reception classes' in
    Adelman, C. Uttering Muttering, Grant MacIntyre
    Ltd 1981

TRANSCRIPTION SYMBOLS

( )	untranscribable or doubtful
(( ))	transcriber's description
//	next utterance overlaps at this point
- - -	untimed pause
:	elongated syllable
hh	aspiration

Chapter Three

HARD TIMES IN RELIGIOUS EDUCATION

Jack W G Hogbin and John R Bailey

SOME PROBLEMS

Major dilemmas continue to face those involved in
Religious Education despite forty years of development since 1944. A substantial body of theory has
offered educational justifications for its place in
the school curriculum, and a rationale for its practice has been articulated. Some would claim that
a consensus on why, what and how to teach RE has
been achieved. They are mistaken. At the chalk-
face, there is widespread disagreement among teachers. The public are confused or highly critical of
what is taught or the purposes of teaching it.
Humanists are divided between outright opponents
and cautious supporters. Members of ethnic minority
communities are in some cases anxious and even hos-
tile.   Recent headlines in the Times Educational
Supplement have read: 'Welsh RE staff admit to
evangelical aims' and 'Muslim censure for London's
RE syllabus'. A consensus cannot be taken for
granted.
      Those who exercise leadership in the subject-
inspectors, advisers, specialist teachers and others-
need to develop responses that are not based simply
on a determination to persuade critics to accept a
supposed consensus that operates as a kind of un-
official orthodoxy. The Muslim rejection of a
syllabus which presents religion as 'an anthropological phenomenon divorced from belief in almighty
God' would be shared by many other faiths. At the
same time, RE ought not to succumb to the lunatic
fringe that regards the fire at York Minster as
a judgement of God upon a church that condones heresy.
The centrality of commitment, the importance of
claims to truth and the meaning of phrases like
open-minded tolerance have still to be debated with

depth and rigour. What are teachers' expectations of pupil response to the claims of religion? If teachers of RE are, on the one hand, not aiming to bring about faith in pupils nor, on the other hand, are they teaching in order to make children agnostics what kind of response is expected? The public have long expected RE to keep order in the streets, to keep pupils off sex and drugs and to endorse values and a life-style that society as a whole has abandone (if it were ever adopted). The public expectations of RE are often quite unrealistic but are a dim recognition of the importance of virtue and a vague expression of a guilt that needs to be removed. Consequently, public institutions including Parliament often declare the overwhelming importance of RE, while failing to will the means to ensure its effectiveness. A recent report from the RE Council quotes more than a dozen statements in five major Government reports since 1977 declaring the importance of RE[1]. The same report uses published DES statistics to demonstrate that the staffing of RE in schools is already poorer than any other subject in the curriculum. The report describes the many faces of shortage, referring to unfilled vacancies in schools ('the periphery of a gaping hole!'), the worse degree of mismatch between specialist qualifications and subject teaching than any other subject, the overloading of RE staff timetables or above average class sizes, and the underprovision of teaching time.

In other quarters, debates first voiced in 1944 rumble on. There are those who question the compulsory nature of RE. In a secular society, where citizens may be as ignorant of Christianity as they are of any other religion, it is a remarkable fact that RE is at present the only legally compulsory subject in the school curriculum. Teachers of the subject themselves disagree on the matter of compulsion. Some argue that since there are good educational justifications for the subject, legal compulsion is unnecessary and produces an adverse reaction among other teachers and many pupils. Other teachers adopt an opposite standpoint and fear for the continued existence of RE if the subject were to face the full rigours of the curriculum market place without legal protection. A new twist to the legal provision for the subject has emerged in recent years. The unique status of RE has been marked since 1870 by the right of parents to withdraw their children from lessons in the subject. For decades this right reflected a recognition of the rivalry

34

between Christian denominations. More recently, parents have withdrawn children because they object to the teaching of 'all those foreign religions', a response to a major change in thinking about the subject, namely from an exclusive focus on Christianity to a multi-faith approach to the study of several world religions.

A major issue, as yet unsolved, is the place of Christianity in relation to the study of other religions. The debate concerns the question: is Britain a Christian country or a multi-faith community? On the one hand are those who argue that from a historical point of view Christianity has been the major force influencing western culture. British culture, it is argued, cannot be understood apart from Christianity and the task of teachers is to transmit that Christian culture to children through the medium of Religious Education in schools. Consequently, Christianity should be the dominant content of the RE syllabus. On the other hand there are those who point out that Britain is a pluralist society, part of a pluralist world, where people belong to a wide variety of religious traditions or even none at all. This pluralism of belief, attitudes and values is said to imply that all systems of belief should receive equal treatment in an objective, fair and balanced syllabus. Emphasis on Christianity risks accusations of racism; equal treatment of religion risks accusations of lack of respect for the British cultural heritage.

Anxieties are widespread. Some ethnic minorities feel that their identities are threatened by the dominant culture and RE is perceived, whether rightly or wrongly, as a danger. Christians feel themselves to be a minority, threatened on the one hand by secularism and on the other by alternative religious traditions. Other people, not necessarily to be identified with any formal religious or ideological tradition, are anxious at the loss of traditional social values and express the view that 'something ought to be done' without knowing just what that 'something' is.

That 'something' has been described as referring to the great existential questions of life and death: why are we here, what is the purpose of life, how ought I to live, why do people suffer, what happens when we die, and is there life after death? These are questions that have been addressed by the great religious and ideological traditions over the centuries. The arts, music, literature and drama, are rich in the exploration of these fundamental

35

questions. Adolescence is understood as a critical stage in every individual's personal development during which an individual's own identity is produced very much in response to these issues. Yet there is considerable evidence that Religious Education has in many instances failed to help pupils to explore these matters in helpful and convincing ways. The most widely expressed response is that the subject is dull and boring, its relevance is not perceived and the standpoints expressed are regarded as old fashioned. Not only are pupils turned off Religious Education, but they are turned off most subjects at school. Surveys of attitudes among secondary school pupils reveal a strong utilitarian approach to school. RE is not regarded as useful and in the popularity stakes the subject is very often near the bottom of the list. The economic crisis that threatens a permanent high level of unemployment presents a widespread threat to the existing structure of schools and a crisis in the traditional curriculum, of which RE is a part.

Changes in the school curriculum seek to respond to many of these issues and may be perceived as a threat or an opportunity depending upon the teacher's position and perspective in the situation. The widespread concern over the sense of values in life and the responsibilities of schools in this respect has led to the development of what is sometimes called 'Personal and Social Education'(PSE). This new area of the curriculum may include not only Religious Education but subsumes careers education, health education, physical education, aspects of literature, history and art, study skills and social studies. Prominent areas for inclusion are also personal relationships, life skills, moral education, consumer education and home management, community studies and community service. No wonder that in-clusion in PSE is often perceived by RE teachers as a threat since the distinctively religious perspec-tive may all too easily become peripheral or even disappear. Resources may quickly be overstretched when facing the demands implicit in such a catalogue of needs. Seen in terms of curriculum content, the result is an attempt to force a gallon into a pint pot. What is RE to do faced with this situation? Should RE teachers oppose PSE, seek an alliance with it, or ignore it as a passing fashion?

RELIGIOUS EDUCATION IN THREE SCHOOLS

The crisis in RE is many sided and a hard look at

what is happening to the subject in schools and the direction in which it should seek to move must be very carefully considered. In order to explore some of the issues involved one author visited three large urban comprehensive schools in a city in the north west of England. He talked to the teachers about the social context of their schools, their general outlook and policies and their perceptions of RE within the practical teaching context. The issues involved present themselves sharply in the following pen portraits of the teachers in these schools.

The portraits are written in an attempt to represent faithfully the ethos and approach of the schools themselves rather than to fit an artificial analytical scheme. Nevertheless, in each case attention will be paid to the social environment of the school, the characteristics of the pupils, the school ethos, the specific approach to RE and the status of the subject. Too often, writers have prescribed an approach to the subject without a sensitive regard for the constraints and opportunities presented by the social and curricular contexts in which teaching must take place.

CLIPPERS GREEN

Clippers Green is an 11-18 girls comprehensive school with easy access to inner city areas. The school is multi-racial. A third of the girls are Asians, mostly Pakistani Muslims, a quarter from a Caribbean background and the remainder are white from a variety of social backgrounds.

Miss B, their teacher, indicated that there was evidence from time to time of racial tension between ethnic groups; for example, between Hindus and Muslims and between the minority of white girls and the majority of pupils from the various ethnic communities. Miss B spoke of the staff awareness of a latent violence underlying the social context of the school and took the view that when violence erupted, racial conflict became a vehicle for the expression of feelings that were not fundamentally racial. She observed that racial conflict appeared to arise 'by accident' at times, for example, after a period when the whole school underwent examinations and pupils were suddenly released from the pressures of a long period of constraint. Few formal disciplinary arrangements existed in the school and staff were very much left to 'fend for themselves'. This lack of support placed a heavy burden on individual

pupil-teacher relationships. Discipline in the
school depended upon a few experienced teachers with
strong individual personalities. Younger, less
experienced teachers faced a situation which containe
difficulties that could erupt without warning.

Turning to the religious standpoints of the
pupils, Miss B commented that most pupils regarded
themselves as belonging to a particular faith
tradition, but the majority knew very little about
their claimed religious heritage. Among coloured
pupils, she observed, in general pupils belonging
to 'mainstream' religious traditions came from
middle class backgrounds, while those from more
'fundamentalist' groups came from poorer working
class families. White pupils defined themselves
as Christian in contrast to the different religious
traditions of pupils of indigenous origin. Miss B
remarked that the stereotype of Asian girls as
passive and conformist compared with other ethnic
groups was no longer accurate, probably because
most of these pupils were born and raised in the UK
and had long exposure to white British culture.
In Miss B's view, the school had no formal policy
with regard to race relations, although the LEA
would claim to have one for all its schools.

Miss B had come several years ago to Clippers
Green from teaching in another northern city. She
had inherited a staff of two and the RE department
had remained at this size for several years although
her staff had changed in terms of individuals. Miss
B described her teaching in her previous school as
teaching religion exemplified by Christianity. Since
coming to Clippers Green she had broadened her approa
to cover a range of religions. She had invested muc
personal time in gaining the broader base of knowledg
necessary and taught an 'A' level course with a
major RE component of Islam. In terms of school
policy, the RE department, like others, relied heavil
on the benevolence of the headteacher. Information
was not readily available regarding logistics, for
example, the number of pupils in examination groups
for each sixth form subject. Miss B and her staff
felt that RE was regarded as peripheral to the
curriculum because the subject was allocated only one
period per class per week. Music, in contrast, had
been given two periods.

RACE, RELIGION AND CULTURE

Clippers Green is a school whose RE staff recognise
the value and importance of a multi-faith approach

to the study of religion. The diverse ethnic
composition of the school demands such an approach.
Even though the largest single group of pupils would
identify themselves as Christians within the Church
of England tradition, there exists a significant
prssure not only of other world religions, but of
minority sects whether Caribbean Pentecostals,
Jehovah's Witnesses, or Seventh Day Adventists.
It is often taken for granted that white pupils are
mostly secular and that pupils from ethnic minorities
are religious. What is clear from talking to pupils
in such multi-ethnic schools is that many pupils,
whether white or black, are ignorant of even basic
information about religion. The children of parents
who were the first generation of immigrants into
the UK are in many cases no less secularised than
their white counterparts. In a class discussion of
religions in Britain, girls were discovering religious
identities - 'She's Baptist Miss', 'I'm non-denomina-
tional' (meant as believing in God but not belonging
to a specific religious tradition or community),
'What does Atheist mean, Miss?' 'Are you Jewish,
Miss?'.

The implicit view expressed by the majority of
pupils was (whatever their claimed religious loyalty)
that one religion was very much as good as another
and that none of them made much difference to the way
one lived one's life. The anxieties of leaders in
the religious traditions may not be entirely un-
founded. Conversations between one author and
individual Muslim girls indicated not only the
importance of religion in terms of cultural identity,
but also the difference between their outlook and
that of their parents who were perceived as 'more
religious'. While this classroom experience indicates that pupils may indeed be 'engaged in a
personal search for meaning purpose and values',
the search is not so much between different
religious traditions as between any religious
tradition and a set of implicit values and beliefs
of a secular kind. Secular beliefs are perceived
as the white British cultural tradition. The
multi-racial school is one where pupils can become
conscious of the 'less immediately obvious values
in the civilisation to which they are heirs', but
they are heirs to more than one civilisation and
it is not necessarily the traditional religious
values that are of uppermost significance. When
pupils in the process of growing up encounter a
variety of faiths and cultures they appear to
engage in a creative cultural process. The

39

religious and cultural heritage is not merely confirmed or rejected, but developed in new ways.
Formal school and informal social processes of education interrelate. Schools like Clippers Green
challenge everyone concerned with Religious Education
to understand the role of the subject in matters of
race relations. Religious beliefs and attitudes
are seldom separate in people's lives from the wider
range of beliefs, attitudes and values. Indeed,
those beliefs, whether religious or secular, to
which we are deeply committed, underpin most other
beliefs, attitudes and values. Beliefs and atti-
tides may be racist in that one racial group
regards itself as superior to others and regards
others in negative ways. Religious and secular
beliefs regarding humankind, may, sometimes deliberately and sometimes unwittingly, lend support to
such standpoints. Such racist attitudes may parallel the attitudes of one religion to another,
where one religion regards itself as exclusive and
superior to others. Such claims need to be distinguished from claims to a unique cultural and
religious heritage, and from any glib denial
of fundamental differences between religions and
cultures. Loyalty to one's religious and
cultural heritage is compatible with mutual respect
and appreciation of others. People of different
race, religion and culture need to be ready to
learn from one other's history, culture, beliefs
and experiences. The insight into the fundamentally
different beliefs, attitudes and values of another,
can lead one into a deeper, firmer, more humane and
just grasp of one's own religious and cultural
identity. Affirmation and criticism of one's
religious and cultural heritage are both necessary
in the process of creative personal and social
development. It is the task of Religious Education
to participate in this process not simply at the
level of direct exposure of racist language and
actions but at a deeper level. Religious Education,
dealing with the search for 'meaning, purpose and
values' may enable pupils to explore their own
feelings and those of others in an open, tolerant,
critical and creative way that can indirectly
contribute far more than would be achieved by
direct confrontation.

ASTOR'S TREES

The situation of Clippers Green is, however very
different from that of other city schools only a

few miles away. Astor's Trees is a mixed eight-form comprehensive school (11-16) developed from a former secondary modern. Mr A described the catchment area of his school as a housing development of 60,000 people, predominantly working class families. The geographical location of the housing development with 'natural' boundaries (green belt, park etc) on all sides helped to produce a strong insularity of outlook among the pupils. The children did not travel to other parts of the city, let alone further afield.

Mr A regarded the area as severely deprived and characterised the pupils as 'survivors'. He observed that pupils generally expected to go from school to Youth Training Schemes or further education of some kind. Most expected eventually to find some kind of employment. He expressed the opinion that the pupils expectations of employment were illusory and feared that if the truth were generally recognised by his pupils, the school would face severe difficulties.

Mr A indicated that the area had only a small number of ethnic minority groups, mostly third or fourth generation, 'middle class shop-keeper', or 'small business families'. The largest and dominant group were white working class families. From his observations of pupils, Mr A perceived clear evidence of latent and occasionally explicit racial prejudice and sensed a subterranean violence. There was, he pointed out, very little overt evidence of violence, telephone boxes were not vandalised unlike some areas. The school did not, said Mr A, find itself in any difficulties, since there was a strong pastoral system, parallel to the academic system, and inter-relating at several points.

The ethos of the school was perceived by Mr A to have changed over a period of time. Emphasis had moved from social aims and pastoral concern to more academic ambitions, limited by an intake of pupils heavily weighted towards the lower end of the ability range. Currently, the emphasis was on developing basic skills, communication skills and life-skills.

Mr A justified Religious Education in academic terms and favoured an objective and broad multi-faith approach. He regarded the study of world religions as appropriate because it was essential to the nature of the subject and in his view met the needs of pupils in his school. He supported a Mode 3 CSE syllabus on these lines, although it was not offered in the school, and he also favoured, with

some reservations, the AEB 'O' level multi-faith
syllabus. Reductions in the staff time available
were claimed to be the reason for not offering
either. He drew attention to the deprivation of
pupils, already mentioned, especially the lack of
cultural or literary support in the home and
recollected that he had, in the past, paid careful
attention to the language needs of his pupils.
He regarded Religious Education as a 'literary'
subject but said that pressures on his time prevented
attention to the difficulties pupils faced in
handling religious language in a multi-faith approach
to the subject.

Mr A's base is in the Lower School. He had
previously taught in several city schools and was
appointed Head of Religious Studies in his present
school prior to re-organisation in 1982. He
felt that RE lost status in 1982 because two full-
time specialist staff were reduced to one and the
subject was no longer available as an examination
option at 16+. He regarded this situation as not
untypical of schools in the City. Mr A regarded the
loss of status of RE as the result not only of re-
organisation brought about by falling rolls but also
as a consequence of the introduction of Personal
and Social Education (PSE) as a curriculum subject
and the innovation of a programme of alternative
curriculum strategies for a sizeable group of under-
achievers. In his view the new programme's claim
to incorporate RE in terms of Personal and Social
Education and Contemporary Studies were not borne
out in practice. Nevertheless, Mr A welcomed the
introduction of PSE although it was largely responsible for loss of time in his subject. The
reduction in timetable hours for RE had enabled
him to use the time available for the distinctively
religious aspects of RE while leaving wider social
and moral issues to others. The reduced number
of teaching hours for RE also enabled time release
for Head of Year duties. Mr A pointed out that in
1982 he had been made Head of Year. He felt that
promotion on the 'pastoral ladder' was his only way
forward in terms of professional development and
he recognised that RE could be said to have suffered
as a result. He recognised that the absence of 16+
examinations in the subject had as much to do with
demands upon his time as other factors. Nevertheless, he pointed out, through the personal support
of the previous head teacher and his long established
position in the school, RE was adequately resourced.
The subject was allocated only one period a week

42

overall (in practice, double periods for fewer weeks).
Double periods were he said, educationally preferable.
Mr A added that his lessons were at times interrupted
by urgent business that arose from his duties as Head
of Year and the longer time span of a lesson minimised
the disruptive effects of such events. Mr A felt that
he could not know how his pupils responded to RE but
that this would be more readily perceived by external
observers rather than himself. While he felt personally secure, he readily agreed that if he were to
leave the school, RE would be in a very vulnerable
position.

RELIGIOUS EDUCATION AND THE PERSONAL QUEST

Astor's Trees like Clippers Green has a multi-faith
approach to RE. While the adoption of this approach
is seen as relating to the pupil's social context
and there is a strong awareness of the existence of
racial prejudice, the approach to RE does not address
itself directly to the experience of the pupils.
Pupils do not identify themselves as Christian or as
generally religious but are secularised within a white
working class context where religion is a peripheral
matter. The approach, characteristic of many schools,
offers a type of RE that if anything widens the gap
between pupils'own experience and the major religious
traditions. Religion is all too readily perceived
as 'academic' and 'remote' with little direct impact
on daily life or the matters of urgent concern to
youngsters. How can RE teachers encourage respect
for people who are different, when the style of RE
offered does not respect the experience and feelings
of the pupils? The separation of the distinctive
features of religion from wider social and moral
concerns itself indicates the nature of the gap.
Religious experience at the heart of the traditions
has never been separated from such matters. While
RE ought not to confine itself to the limited secular
experience of pupils, neither can it afford to
neglect that experience or fail to bring it into
a critical relationship with the traditions.
      One of the major reasons for the failure of the
subject to come to grips with these issues is well
illustrated by an inspection of the RE syllabus
at Astor's Trees, a syllabus typical of many in
English schools. The syllabus begins with a first
year study of God(s), Founders, Worship, Places of
Worship, Scriptures, Festivals and Codes of Belief
covering five major religions: Judaism, Christianity, Hinduism, Sikhism, Buddhism. The second year

43

offers a study of Christianity which is studied in
terms of the life of Jesus, the spread of Christianity and how Christianity came to be divided. The
third year in the Autumn and Spring terms currently
studies world religions (third year pupils followed
a different first year course) and in the summer
term considers the theme of 'Myself and Others' in
which a series of moral/social issues involving
personal relationships, group relationships, work,
leisure and money are considered. The syllabus is
dominated by subject content on a vast scale.
Syllabuses of this kind reflect changes in the
subject over the last twenty years - each new fashion
adds a further layer of content to be covered. The
absurdity is evident when one thinks of the vast range that is to be taught in one or two thirty-five
minute periods over three years. The syllabus pattern
also conveys a spurious consensus. Each approach to
the subject implicit in a different area of content,
if understood, contradicts another in important ways.
There are, moreover, significant implications for
teaching method that are ignored. At another level,
particular religious traditions are accepted author-
itatively and themselves are all too easily presented
with a spurious unity that fails to recognise the
differences, anxieties and uncertainties within each
one. In religious terms, any one tradition may itself
claim an absolute, unchanging validity as some kind
of special revelation. While there is no doubt that
RE is involved in the transmission of a religious
and cultural heritage, that heritage is not to be
understood as a static, monolithic body of knowledge
which deserves respect at the expense of respect for
the contemporary experience of pupils. As the
Berkshire Agreed syllabus puts it, the religious
heritage must be related to the personal quest². The
difficulties faced by RE are perhaps an acute version
of difficulties experienced across a wide spectrum
of the conventional school curriculum. Gabriel
Chanon and Linda Gilchrist express the matter
perceptively when they write:

> In conventional education we find a pre-
> dominant image of the past as static,
> either because it is 'finished' as in
> the presentation of history, or because
> it is 'external', as in the presentation
> of literature and art. We do not find
> much attempt to understand the past as
> it was experienced at the time - that is,
> as being full of doubt, dispute and danger,

as the present is to us. We find
little recognition of the fact that
our awareness of the past is our vicarious
experience of other people's present.[3]

A multi-faith approach to RE needs to recognise that
the heritage of the past is always revalued in the
present. While the gulf exists between RE teachers
who are dominated by respect for the past and pupils
whose adolescent development sharpens their awareness
of the present and the future that lies before them,
the processes of finding a relevant appropriation
of the traditional religious and cultural heritage
cannot take place. The traditions and the experience
of teachers and pupils need to address more explicitly
the great universal questions not in terms of large
quantities of information to be passively absorbed
but as processes of insight and criticism, of enquiry
and empathy, of expression and interpretation, of
confident open-mindedness and critical commitment.
Such processes demand that the experiences and
thoughts of pupils are central rather then peripheral
to RE. Although the aims of the syllabus at Astor's
Trees may be to assist pupils in a 'personal search
for meaning, purpose and values'[4] the contents of the
scheme itself bring into question whether the declared
aims are matched by appropriate practice.   The personal quest. may at times be more readily evident
in Personal and Social Education than in RE. Fears
that the distinctive character of RE could be lost
in a merger with PSE must be balanced by a fear that
RE outside PSE may increasingly lack relevance and
meaning for the lives of pupils.   The personal
quest may, however, easily take place in an
entirely secular context devoid of the challenge
of any religious belief.   Many of these issues are
raised with equal or greater sharpness in the pen
portrait of the third school.

BENNETT'S PLACE

Bennett's Place is a school not unlike Astor's Trees
in many respects. The school is another eight form
entry, 11-16 mixed comprehensive two or three miles
from the city centre. The pupils are mostly white,
from working class families with little contact in
school with ethnic minority pupils. Mr S, the Head
of RE, expressed the view that pupils regularly
exhibited strong racial prejudice in school and
overtly racial incidents were not entirely unknown
in the local area. The pupils lived in a culture

that gave a high valuation to soccer, pop-music,
television and unemployment.   The TV news, however,
was for most pupils time to move from the chair
for a cup of tea. Mr S regarded the cultural
world of his pupils as far removed from his own and
by implication inferior to his own middle class
standards.   He regarded the school curriculum
as a matter of knowledge, emphasised the importance
of basic skills such as reading, writing and
mathematics and deprecated the trendy fashions of
education. Mr S believed that the structure of the
school in mixed ability groups was an outcome of
political decisions rather than educational principle
and that this structure produced major problems of
pupil control. In his view every class contained a
few disruptive pupils who necessitated much time and
attention on his part and distracted him from the
real job of teaching.   Mr S was unhappy with any
suggestion that RE should be part of a Humanities
scheme with team teaching. He was equally suspicious
of PSE which he thought attempted too much and
emphasised pupil's self-expression at the expense
of basic skills or the acquisition of subject
knowledge.   He believed in rigorous subject specialism.   The view was expressed by Mr S that RE was
accorded low status in the school and he felt isolate
He could not envisage a lifetime's career in RE at
the chalk face and hoped vaguely for future promotion
out of the classroom. Meanwhile he had adopted a mult
faith approach to RE and was developing a class libra
of textbooks, religious artefacts and audio-visual
aids in order to teach more effectively.
     Elsewhere in the same school, outside RE, much
PSE work took place. Here is just one example. A
group of fourth year pupils involved in a programme o
alternative curriculum strategies were spending a
morning engaged in drama/PSE activities. A group
of unemployed youngsters on a further education
course presented a series of four dramatic scenes
for discussion: a family quarrel over an unemployed
daughter's attempts to become a garage mechanic,
family reactions to the daughter's return from
unsuccessful job interviews, the family response to
the daughter's subsequent shop lifting and the
family's final reaction to the daughter securing
a temporary job with a pop group. Discussions
involved consideration of attitudes to parental
authority, sex stereotyping, the motives for
stealing and its possible consquences, issues of self
respect and seeing other people's point of view, as
well as practical matters such as techniques involved

in being interviewed for a job. After a coffee
break, the fourth year class divided into small
groups to develop role-plays arising from the
situation analysed earlier.
     These activities in PSE are firmly based in
pupils' own experience or are experiences with which
they could easily identify. The social and moral
concerns that permeate the learning could be said
to exemplify an approach that inherits those
concerns traditionally exercised by Religious
Education. While matters of belief, attitude and
value are deeply involved, the framework is noticeably
secular. We may also question whether there is an
implicit intention to enable pupils to adjust to the
social situation rather than establish some kind of
critique of the social status quo. Among some
teachers and members of the public,mention of such a
critique can act like a red rag to a bull and elicit
fears of overt political influence. However, a
more deeply critical perspective on a different
basis is possible, where a religious perspective is
brought to bear upon social and moral issues. In
this case, the derivation of the work-ethic from
the Protestant Christian tradition, the western
family assumptions deriving from a similar Christian
tradition and consideration of perspectives from
other religious traditions and their implications for
changing patterns of life style could have been a
valuable contribution in terms of subsequent development and analysis. For Religious Education, therefore, there arise a number of issues: what is the
balance between informational knowledge of other
faiths and cultures and the existential quest for
meaning, purpose and values; how do the two perspectives interrelate in the secular, pluralistic
context of urban schools; and what is to be the
curricular and organisational relationship between
Religious Education and Personal and Social Education?

THE 'CINDERELLA' SUBJECT

In each of the three schools visited, the status of
RE is in question. The subject appears to attempt
too much in too short a time and its importance in
the curriculum is belied by the position it occupies.
The teachers have low morale and are oppressed by
the need for survival, whether as teachers of
a viable subject or as professional individuals
engaged in a life-time career. RE teachers feel
professionally isolated but could at times be said
to be their own worst enemy. The strength and

weakness of RE in any school is largely dependent
(whatever the legal position) on the personal
attitude of headteachers and the individual strength
or weakness of the specialist in the subject, who is
often the only specialist in the school. Few RE
departments would claim to possess the 5 per cent
share of resources regarded as the sum necessary for
the effective provision of the subject. Falling
rolls in secondary schools make the subject more vulnerable. These three schools each had a trained spec
ialist head of department but each faces acute problems. Only one of the three schools had more than
one full time RE teacher. It is not uncommon to find
schools that expect a solitary RE specialist to teach
over 600 pupils per week. It is paradoxical that
while students who have completed four years of specialist initial teacher training in RE cannot get jobs
the provision in schools is gravely inadequate. More
over, nearly 60 per cent of all teachers teaching RE
have no qualifications in the subject. At the level
of logistics there can be no doubt that RE is facing
a crisis and becoming a Cinderella subject. The
crisis is not, however, merely a logistical one.
Equally grave is the question of the quality of
teaching in the subject. The lack of specialists
points towards the problem of quality. The investigation at the practical level into these schools,
however limited in terms of scope and number, has
raised basic questions regarding the fundamental
teaching strategies commonplace in the subject.

THE WAY FORWARD

Throughout this chapter there has been frequent
reference to the relationship between RE and PSE.
There are both dangers and opportunities present
in this relationship. Major government funds are
being poured into the development of PSE. RE has
to soldier on. There are dangers that RE may lose
its distinctive identity and contribution to
pupils' personal development. At its worst, RE
and PSE could become not only competitors for
scarce resources, but also the field of ideology,
PSE expressing a secular humanistic ideology,
RE expressing an ideology of religious commitment.
In these circumstances, RE could over time disappear
as its Cinderella status worsens rather than be
abolished by deliberate act of legislation. Indeed,
it is possible to argue that PSE has emerged as a
result of the very weakness of Religious Education
in the school curriculum.

There is, however, a positive scenario that could be developed if schools have the courage to take the initiative. The positive scenario looks towards a close relationship between Religious Education and Personal and Social Education. RE must rigorously pursue its declared aim of enabling pupils to engage in 'a personal search for meaning, purpose and values'. There is some evidence that the different social context of some urban schools may inhibit the strong pursuit of this aim. Schools in such situations may often present difficult problems of control; the fear of social, moral and religious controversy sparking off major disruption may lead RE into safer antiquarian concerns and PSE may be unconsciously led to focus on an implicit policy of social adjustment. The crisis in RE is perhaps best understood as one expression of a wider social crisis. 'Comfortable Britain', the Britain of the better off middle class,[6] wants a safe and comfortable RE that supports established values in a Christian affluent society. A token attention to other faiths and cultures gilds the lily. If attempts to provide the core of a social critique, then we are told religion should keep out of politics and social questions. Comfortable Christians too quickly forget that Christ was crucified for offering a religious and moral critique of the society and culture he lived in while affirming his identity as a member of that society. Other faiths are of central importance in that it is not enough to offer a critique but there is a need for consideration of alternative values and changes in life style. Christians need have no fear of such challenges. When faith speaks to faith in a social critique of contemporary culture and commitments each may be drawn to rediscover that which is truly human in the particular religious and cultural tradition to which its members belong.

To understand the divine is to discover a fresh view of humanity. We are challenged to adopt new values and reject our implicit assumptions. While such changes will not necessarily provide precise solutions to our social problems, the changes will activate those attitudes and dispositions that are favourable towards the eventual discovery of effective responses to them. We shall think differently when we bring ourselves to a greater awareness of the technological abuses of our human resources and environment, our conventional attitudes towards human violence and warfare and our ways of life in which greater priority is given to ruthless individualism than to more co-operative and mutually supportive less competitive personal relationships. These matter ought to be of urgent concern to Religious Education and education in general. They are, however, deeply disturbing both to comfortable Britain and to the established pattern of educational practice. Teachers of RE have a responsibility to help pupils engage in creative dialogue and analysis.

In crude terms, RE must try as a first step, to become less exclusively cerebral and more practical. A key to a more practical approach that gives rise to reflective critical and analytical thinking, is to provide more opportunity for direct personal contributions to work in RE. As the Clippers Green CSE syllabus declares:

> The work of the following terms will involve at least one visit to a place of worship connected with each of the religious groups so far studied, the meeting of a representative outside school from each of the religions; the beginning of an individual piece of work from each girl entitled 'This is our Life'. This will show how much religion makes provision for the major stages of our lives, e.g. birth, adolescence, marriage, death. Wherever possible, the experience of individuals within the group will be called upon to benefit the whole group.

Such an approach not only provides experience for pupils, which may be lacking in their secularised situation, but enables those with a religious/cultural background to use their faith as a basis from which to develop the opportunity for greater personal awareness of their own heritage. Where such experience is linked with class discussion and course work, provision for dialogue between different beliefs, attitudes and values can occur. The scope exists for language both oral and written to be used in a context of inquiry and reflection rather than simply as a means of factual recording or description. Such approaches would normally be expected to be part of school life from topic work in primary school to project work at 16+. A recent and valuable addition to these approaches are the provision of urban trails where pupils make a study visit to a local community (not simply a place of worship) where religion may be seen as part of the cultural life of a community, e.g. the Chinese or Jewish

50

communities in the City. The provision of such experience is especially important for pupils whose experience is as insular as that of the pupils as Astor's Trees. Indeed, the accepted division of experience into sacred and secular so readily taken for granted in western industrial societies is not the normal pattern in others. Asian cultures, for example Indian and Chinese, are permeated by religious tradition.

The recognition of the importance of religious experience and practice in the lives of others may help pupils to question its absence in their own lives. At a deeper level, the different values and beliefs encountered will sharpen and clarify their awareness of their own unrecognised assumptions of beliefs, attitudes and values. In particular, the pupil may come to recognise that contemporary British society raises fundamental questions of compassion, justice and equality that have long been part of the western heritage but have continuing relevance for each one of us whatever our race, creed or political persuasion. The use of religion in the construction of a sense of community is one important challenge that Religious Education in alliance with PSE may make to the anomic, depersonalised and alienated individuals to be found so frequently in different urban areas. Residential experiences, simulation, role-play and the greater use of the media of the creative arts offer similar opportunities for experience, reflection and practical action that might characterise such an alliance. Teachers who question the practical possibilities of such approaches for the single specialist teaching RE one period per week may well consider the opportunities offered by a positive approach as part of, or in conjunction with Personal and Social Education. Indeed, the far reaching implications of pupils' moral and social development as a major aspect of the curriculum ought not to and cannot be met by any one subject alone. It is up to specialist teachers of Religious Education to grasp the nettle; had they been willing to do so with vigour and skill in earlier years. PSE might never have emerged as a potential rival.

Seen in this way RE may yet become a force to be reckoned with. If education is regarded as cultural revaluation, then RE can provide the substance of spirituality in its broadest sense that makes a better future a possibility rather than a remote hope.[7]

REFERENCES

1. Religious Education Provision 1984. RE
Council 1984.
2. Religious Heritage and Personal Quest,
Guidelines for Religious Education, Royal County
of Berkshire 1982
3. Gabriel Chanan & Linda Gilchrist, What
School is For, Methuen and Co., 1974
4. This phrase is derived from 'The Agreed
Syllabus of Religious Education, Hampshire Education
Authority, 1978
5. The Management of Religious Education in the
Secondary School. A CEM Report 1979
6. The Bishop of Liverpool, the Rt. Rev. David
Sheppard used this term in the BBC's 1984 Dimbleby
Lecture
7. The names of individuals and schools in
this chapter are fictitious. The authors are
entirely responsible for the views expressed.

Chapter Four

PERSONAL AND SOCIAL EDUCATION FOR ALL: APART OR
TOGETHER?

David Hustler and Ian Ashman

THE PROBLEM

Our problem in this paper is in general terms a very
old one: it is to do with who gets what sort of
curriculum.   The specific area we are concerned with
is 'personal and social education', and our focus
will be on developments for 14 to 16 year olds.   We
will set out three possible scenarios for the future
of personal and social education programmes for this
age-group.   In our view only one of these futures
is worth fighting for, and it so happens to be the
one which we feel is the most unlikely candidate for
success.   Our commitment is to the growth of personal and social education programmes which bring
together pupils of differing abilities and orientations, programmes which require pupils with differing pasts, and probably differing futures in our
society, to relate to one another.   The small growth
towards such programmes is, we believe, under threat
and here lies our crisis: a crisis which demands
action from those who share our commitments.
     Although this paper is clearly not presented
as an empirical exercise in the traditional sense,
it does stem from a particular set of involvements
which the authors have had.   It is our interactions
with particular schemes, particular LEAs, with
particular young people and particular teachers and
schools - all in the North West - which provide the
basis for this article.   Pointing up some of these
relationships in autobiographical outline may lead
the reader to find it a distinctive or peculiarly
narrow basis.   It has however been our everyday professional lives which have led to these views: in
this sense the paper parallels other contributions
to this book.   We have not gone out of our way to
'find' additional support for the argument and we

will, in this paper, make little reference to the
wide range of literature on such issues.   In short,
it might be said that our position has developed
through a particular, if most basic, form of experiential learning.

One author, trained as a teacher, worked for
a number of years in the Youth Opportunities Programme and the Youth Training Scheme, first as a
teacher of Social and Life Skills, then as a manager
and development worker within the YMCA's 'Training
for Life' scheme.   He is now working in a co-ordinat-
ing and support role with the Manpower and Services
Commission (MSC) training programmes in the London
Borough of Lambeth.   He has been heavily involved
in the development of what is termed Trainee Centred
Reviewing - an approach which has informed recent
'profiling' debates - and is on the Counselling and
Career Development Unit (CCDU) and 'Life Skills
Associates' panels of staff trainers[1].   The latter
has involved him in running courses in life skills
and trainee centred reviewing for teachers and
lecturers.   He has had a particular interest in the
structuring and fruitful development of residential
experiences for young people.

The other author works in teacher education,
having heavy involvements in both pre-service Secondary PGCE courses for intending Social Studies and
PSE teachers, as well as a range of in-service
Courses for practising teachers, including Regional
DES courses.   Related to these involvements are a
range of relationships with PSE and Life Skills
support groups, as well, of course, as relationships
with a variety of schools and their particular
approaches and developments of PSE programmes.   More
recently this author has had an evaluation relationship with Manchester LEA's 'Alternative Curriculum
Strategies' project, for 14-16 year olds.   This
project is one of the several 'Lower Attaining
Pupils' projects, although Manchester has distinctive
long-term aims associated with changing the experience of schooling for a much wider range of pupils.
The project also places considerable emphasis on
processes of personal and social development.

These autobiographical outlines provide the
background to the following observations and argument

PREMATURE OPTIMISM

The curricular area at issue goes by many names:
'education for living';   'social education';   'life
studies';   'personal and social development';   'design

for living'. We are using one of the commonest of
titles: 'personal and social education' in short
PSE. The schemes themselves often draw on an amalgum
of perspectives including concerns relating to Health
Education, Careers Education, Political Education,
Social Studies, Religious Studies. As schemes they
may be more or less integrated, and they certainly
have different emphases in different schools. Some
stress the acquisition of 'citizenship skills', of
what pupils 'need to know' in order to pursue
everyday life after school without unnecessary
difficulties. If these might be thought of by some
as narrowly utilitarian, others which stress the
exploration of personal value positions as these
relate to personal decision-making might be viewed as
extremely individualistic. A further contrast here
is with schemes which orient pupils towards not only
the possibilities for community involvement but also
for group action relating to perceived problems. We
are not going to overview these approaches, nor to
make a case for any one [2]. We also do not intend to
discuss the relative merits of the different organisational modes for implementing such schemes, although we should point to the basic division between
those schools operating programmes as units in
conventional curriculum time, and those which relate
a programme to tutorial structures and the school's
pastoral system. In addition, there is the possibility
of building in an emphasis on personal and social
education across a whole range of curricular activities: this is an important development taken up
later.
     The particular developments we wish to note at
this point have been the moves to some such experience for all pupils, and, increasingly, towards an
experience which is planned and coherent for all.
This represents quite a shift since ROSLA, where we
saw the emergence and in some cases resuscitation
and strengthening of PSE type programmes for the
'less academic' pupil. Such programmes rarely
adopted the teaching and learning relationships
which some would seem to be so central to PSE today
and which we will be discussing later.   Our
point is that planned courses on personal and
social development were usually viewed as appropriate
only for certain types of pupils. In practice,
course titles such as 'social education' were often
only euphemisms for strictly custodial work for the
less academic and the disruptive. The change has
been the move to programmes for all pupils, and recent
LEA guidelines document increasing sources of

pressure on schools in this direction, Manchester
LEA's 'Curriculum for Today and Tomorrow' being one
such example.
      Probably the most useful document discussing the
above movements and pressures is Kenneth David's
Personal and Social Education in Secondary Schools.
What we wish to do is pick up on one aspect of
Kenneth David's definition of PSE. The definition
eventually arrived at is

> Personal and social education includes
> the teaching and informal activities
> which are planned to enhance the
> development of knowledge, understanding,
> attitudes and behaviour, concerned with:
>
> oneself and others;
> social institutions, structures and organisation
> and social and moral issues
>
> (David p.18)

without wishing to see 'oneself and others' as
separate from what follows in this definition,
our interest is in the relationship between this
and a final issue highlighted by Kenneth David prior
to formulating the definition. This reads as follows

> We do not accept that work in personal and
> social education is particularly, or only,
> relevant to the average or below-average
> ability student, and that the more able either
> do not require or cannot spare the time from
> traditional examination subjects for this
> aspect of their education. The implications
> are equally important at all levels of
> education, and have significance for every
> citizen. To curtail this aspect of education
> for more able students is to show a lack of
> educational balance.
>
> (David,p.17)

This quotation brings us to our central commitment.
We would add one crucial additional dimension to
this argument on the importance of PSE for all,
and it is a dimension which many schools have worked
hard to achieve. The addition is that as far as
possible PSE time should bring together pupils
of differing abilities and orientations. It seems
especially important to any worthwhile notion of
PSE in a comprehensive system, that this integration
should obtain during the last two years of mandatory
schooling. Any concern for 'oneself and others'

must surely be pursued in part through relationships with the range of others in the school context before they go their separate ways.

We have briefly traced out some developments in PSE which give many of the teachers we work with and talk to grounds for optimism.   Such courses seem to be escaping their 'ROSLA Child' origins, and several schools have managed to move towards programmes integrating pupils of differing abilities and orientations.   Unfortunately, our view is that this optimism is premature, for there are other currents shaping the PSE prospects for 14-16 year olds.   We concentrate on two currents in particular over the next two sections.

SOCIAL AND LIFE SKILLS: POST 16

The first of these currents is the impact on schools of post-16 developments in the area of 'social and life skills'.   In short this can be described as the rise and fall of social and life skills within MSC sponsored schemes.   The concept of social and life skills was not new at the time, but the 1977 publications by the MSC of their 'Instructional Guide to Social and Life Skills Training' first brought this term into common usage.   This guide was intended to be particularly relevant to those running schemes under the Commission's Work Experience Programme.   The latter was later integrated along with social and life skills into the Youth Opportunity programme.   The label was also adopted by the Unified Vocation Preparation programme which provided basic training for employed young people.

Such schemes, and particularly the Youth Opportunities Programme (YOP), increased the scale of their provision rapidly.   It was within the 'hothouse' context of schemes for 16-19 year olds, particularly the 'non-academic' unemployed, that social and life skills programmes became established as a curricular element for significant numbers of young people.   A massive range of literature, resource materials, and personnel, emerged hand in hand with social and life skills.   The Further Education Curriculum Review and Development Unit (FEU) was particularly prominent in publishing overviews of the area, and the Counselling and Career Development Unit (CCDU) were influential, especially as regards teaching approaches.   We will shortly take up some aspects of their approaches which are central to our argument.   However, having pointed to the 'rise' of social and life skills we need to pursue what we mean by its 'fall', at least in the MSC-sponsored post-16 context.

With the translation of the Youth Opportunities Programme into the Youth Training Scheme (YTS), the opportunity for young people to experience social and life skills seems to have declined rapidly. The phrase 'Social and Life Skills' has virtually disappeared as legitimate vocabulary within YTS. The YTS is divided into different organisational modes with the MSC displaying a distinct preference for the largely employer based schemes.   It so happens that many of the Voluntary agencies, such as the YMCA, had a strong history of involvement in the development of social and life skills and retained such work within YTS, albeit sometimes by a different name.   It also happens that their schemes are much more expensive.   For whatever reasons, it is the case that these schemes have been constrained and cut back since the original inception of YTS.

One central question concerns where the efforts of Social and Life Skills trainers, and these developing resources, are now being directed.   Our experience is that they are increasingly to be found in influencing, training, supporting and teaching in schools.   Certainly there would seem to have been an increasing demand for in-service teacher training in this field.   If schools are where many of the social and life skills trainers are going, we now need to see what approaches they are taking with them.

Our preferred way into this would be to provide details of our own experiences with young people within MSC programmes.   Space limitations constrain us instead to focus briefly on one of the most popular and influential sets of publications in this area.   This is the work emanating from the CCDU and linked to the names of Barrie Hopson and Mike Scally. We are not at all concerned to criticise their publications.   On the contrary, one of the authors has a history of involvement with, and commitment to, their approaches.   The key books are <u>Life Skills Teaching</u> and <u>Life Skills Teaching Programmes I and II</u>. The former makes a powerful general case for their approach in the context of a concern for personal competence and education in post-industrial society.   Its central theme is how a lifeskill based curriculum might help to generate 'self-empowerment' by which they mean 'the process by which one increasingly takes greater charge of oneself and one's life'.   They outline a basic framework for a life skill teaching programme which draws on 'Me: skills

I need to manage and grow' (eg 'how to be positive
about myself') leading into 'Me and you: skills I
need to relate effectively to you', 'Me and others:
skills I need to relate effectively to others', and
Me and specific situations (e.g.'skills I need for
my education'). The book also contains chapters
on life skills teaching in schools and colleges
and lifeskills teaching methods. The Lifeskills
Teaching Programmes I and II contain a massive range
of possible teaching and learning activities tightly
structured in terms of sequential development and
heavily reliant on active experiential learning.
    Approaches such as Hopson and Scally's have
come in for published criticism and we have certainly
experienced similar criticisms. Pursuing one line
of criticism allows us to point to a particularly
important strand within this approach to social and
lifeskills. Bernard Davies's 'In Whose Interests'
criticises the way in which social and lifeskills
training might serve to individualise problems, to
de-politize young people and to hinder an awareness
of the ways in which problems and futures for individuals and groups are structured by systems within
our society. He advocates the retention of his sense
of 'Social Education'. Although not addressed to
Bernard Davies, Hopson and Scally argue that:

> Self empowerment begins with oneself and
> spreads to others; but self-empowered
> behaviour is most effectively developed
> in systems that are structured to encourage,
> reinforce, and teach it. 'Social action or
> self empowerment' is a false dichotomy. People
> can become more self-empowered by learning
> lifeskills, by teachers modelling growth-
> oriented values, and helping students become
> more aware of their internal and external
> worths, by giving them information, by helping
> them develop goals and commitments, but also
> by working to change our schools and other
> institutions into empowering rather than
> depowering places to live and work.

(Life Skills Teaching p.79)

The strand we wish to pick up immediately from this
excerpt is the clear message to schools that they
need to change. They need to change in terms of
fundamental aspects of the relationship between pupils
and teachers. It is this that many see as a core
feature of successful social and lifeskills and which
informs some messages to teachers in the Lifeskills

59

Teaching Programmes referred to earlier. These messages are along the following lines: that pupils need to be given more responsibility for themselves; that much of the teacher's traditional control and power in the classroom needs to be sacrificed if pupils are to develop more personal autonomy; that the traditional classroom settings themselves need to change, since for many pupils such settings already carry strong connotations of subordination and failure.

Although Hopson and Scally's work is addressed to schools, and much of the original piloting was done in schools, the context for most of its early use and success was within Post 16 MSC schemes. Certainly for one of the authors of this paper, it was the perceived success of such approaches within YOP initially, which accelerated his commitment to such social and lifeskills work. In particular, it was with young people who were disaffected with schooling, and brought with them a sense of educational and personal failure, that success was most apparent. Perhaps more than anything else success was visible in terms of some young people becoming 'more aware of their internal and external worths'. It is a matter of conviction for this author that social and lifeskills programmes played a part in these personal developments. It is also a matter of conviction that the relationships were crucial. The methods associated with such approaches demanded distinctive tutor-trainee relationships, and, together with negotiation of programmes and an increasingly trainee centred approach to assessment-cum-reviewing, young people were encouraged to feel accepted as individuals and motivated towards participation and achievement.

We have then identified one central aspect of the social and lifeskills approach: the requirement for distinctive teacher-pupil relationships, certainly running counter to those traditionally experienced in schools. We have also identified a key feature as regards the experience of social and lifeskills within the MSC post-16 schemes: that, for some, such approaches were particularly successful with the 'school failures' and the 'disaffected'. We also note that social and lifeskills trainers do not seem to have such a secure place within YTS and that they and their ideas appear to have receptive audiences in schools. Why this should be so will become apparent in the following section.

14-16 YEAR OLDS: INITIATIVES FOR THE 'LESS ACADEMIC'

The second 'current' shaping prospects for PSE consists of the range of recent initiatives associated with 'disaffected' and 'less-academic' fourteen to sixteen year olds, though these schemes may have a 14-18 span. We are referring here to initiatives such as the MSC's Technical and Vocational Educational Initiatives (TVEI), the DES Lower Attaining Pupils projects, and a variety of smaller LEA and single school sponsored developments. Our focus will be a Manchester's version of the Lower Attaining Pupils (LAP) project, 'Alternative Curriculum Strategies', but we need first to convey our sense of the impact these developments are having on at least some senior personnel in schools.

The MSC's intervention in pre -16 schooling has certainly had its share of publicity. The TVEI schemes are seen by some as an unwarrented intrusion by 'trainers' into the world of 'educationalists'. Whatever one's judgement might be on this, it has been our clear impression that many senior staff in schools have already been influenced in at least one respect: this intervention has served as a renewed stimulus to rethink central aspects of the experience of schooling for many of our pupils.

This theme is captured in the following extract from a booklet of materials generated during a regional DES course directed by one of the authors. Course participants produced brief papers outlining aspects of their own views on course issues, and this extract comes from one Headmaster's account:

"During the course, reference was frequently made to the 'Alternative Curriculum Strategy' espoused by Manchester as a possible answer to the problems of boredom, disaffection and under-achievement experienced by significant numbers of pupils in the 14-16 age range. The word 'Alternative' seems to imply the complete rejection of the current strategies employed for the final two years of statutory schooling whereas it may be more realistic to aim at the gradual incorporation and assimilation of the best new ideas to achieve real progress in the future. It is probably important to remind ourselves continually that we are trying to put relevance and vitality into sections of the curriculum. In many secondary schools, examples of good practice are already in evidence.

With Keith Evans' views on structural employment at the heart of our discussions, it could be helpful for schools to test their own curricular provision for Years 4-5 with the following check-list derived from the speakers' ideas outlined on the course:

> (Keith Evans, Deputy
> Director of Education
> for Clwyd was one of the
> course speakers)

1 Are teachers willing to make a major change of approach by WORKING WITH children to attain agreed goals? Is it possible for covenants between pupils and teachers to be negotiated and formally defined for specified periods of time?

2 Are teachers willing to allow the pupils to find out their own answers, to sift out their own information, to go through the discovery process?

3 Is sufficient use being made of experiential teaching methods? Are the local, out-of-school resources used frequently by the pupils?

4 Is sufficient thought being given to a credentials package for school leavers including a profile and various certificates covering a wide range of activities?

5 Has each pupil the opportunity to participate in a Life and Social Skills programme?

Many staff are programmed to reject automatically the ideas which are implicit in the above questions. Lift-off and development will only occur if committed teachers with leadership qualities are involved, if scale points are allocated by headteachers, if teaching groups are not too large, and finally if there are control mechanisms to ensure that the covenants are adhered to by the pupils and staff.'

Our feeling is that there is a current of
opinion among many teachers that 'traditional
schooling' has failed, and is failing, relatively
large numbers of pupils. For these teachers, the
MSC intervention is not being reacted to with a
'take the money and run' orientation. This, and
other initiatives, are increasingly being seen as
providing possible solutions to a problem: the
problem of the 'under-achieving', the 'low-attaining'
and the 'non-academic' pupils in the current
economic context. Of course in a sense this
problem has always been there as a worry for
teachers. The difference at this time seems to
be the extent to which really quite radical changes
for large numbers of pupils are viewed as being
necessary.
In our view, Manchester's 'Alternative Curriculum Strategies' project incorporates within it many
of these radical changes. As such, it provides us
with what is possibly a preview of developments to
come elsewhere. The project has already received
considerable attention, and is clearly experiencing
some success as well[3] . We focus here only on some
common features operating across what is in fact a
project with variety deliberately built into it
across the involved schools. As was stressed in
the invitation to Manchester Schools to bid for
funds, the aim is to promote radical changes in
the curriculum for 4th and 5th year pupils, and
a different emphasis within schools. The initial
aim of the project is to ensure that those pupils
not reached by current curriculum offerings
are given a fair and coherent alternative 'deal'.
For the pupils who opted in, a large proportion
of the week is spent with a group tutor and in
their own 'base rooms' which have the flavour of
progressive Primary School practice. There is an
emphasis on out of school activities and on mixing
with a range of adults in, for example, community
projects, outdoor pursuits, and work experience.
The stress is on short modular courses with no
long haul for two years towards traditional
exams. Much is made of what might be termed
'pupil-centred reviewing' of progress made and
targets to be achieved, with criterion-referenced
assessment recording skills acquired. Experiential
learning is the sine qua non, and pupils are
involved again and again in making choices, in
negotiating with staff and each other, in making
decisions and taking the responsibility for those
decisions. A central point is that the personal

63

and social education of pupils is viewed as a key
emphasis across a whole range of curricular
activities.
      As the project's original bid to the DES notes,
'The main aim is to create a different milieu in
schools......' and for the initial target groups of
pupils something different does seem to have been
created. An extensive programme of interviewing
and other sources, displays that to date at
least - a year into the project - many pupils do
feel that 'They treat us like adults now', 'It's
better than ordinary school and we're learning
things too', 'You don't have to wag it any more'
'You make your own decisions and teachers talk to
you like real people', 'It's not like lessons'.
      The first year of the project has focussed, not
surprisingly, on motivating the pupils and on personal
and social development across a range of curricular
activities including residential experiences.
Observers might point to the high priority accorded
to the project within the LEA, to the large-scale
resourcing and intensive staff development programmes
and have doubts about future prospects when funding
ends. However, there has been a quite dramatic shift
away from traditional patterns of schooling 14-16,
and the central shift has been in the nature of the
relationship obtaining between teacher and pupil.
Our view is that developments here to date have
much in common with Hopson and Scally's ambition that
schools might become 'empowering' institutions - at
least for these pupils and the teachers most closely
involved with them as well. It is not at all surprising to find personnel with a history of close
involvement with the CCDU and with commitments to the
associated social and life skills approaches, already
attached to the project.
      As we noted much earlier, Manchester has the
long-term aim, associated with this project, of
changing the experience of schooling for all pupils.
This was made clear right from the start in the
invitation for bids. 'But quite quickly it needs to
be the case that schools are enabled to re-fashion
their curriculum offering to the whole of the fourth
and fifth year so that pupils are able to choose
between the alternatives........ The whole idea is
to change and enrich mainstream provision for all
pupils'. In some ways this might be taken to represent a thrust against the chances of an extended
differentiation: on the one side a 'practical
curriculum for practical kids', and on the other
side the same traditional schooling as before.

64

Whether or not Manchester's long term aims will be successful, is of course yet to be seen.   What is undeniable is that those long-term aims are taken seriously by this particular LEA.   At this point our central worry relating to the impact of initiatives such as this project on PSE can be made explicit.   The very success of such initiatives with the 'less academic' and with the 'disaffected' may militate against long-term aims such as Manchester's. Where those long-term aims were never there in the first place, those who share our commitment to integrated PSE programmes will have even more of a fight on their hands.

Both at pre-16 and at post-16 there are of course major 'whole curriculum' developments, such as TVEI and the Certificate of Pre-Vocational Education framework, where personal and social education or the acquisition of social and life skills is given considerable importance.   Despite MSC's attempts to broaden the ability range of its target groups for TVEI, clear-cut alternative routes are being rapidly established for the 'less academic'. The major schemes are mirrored by many smaller developments, some linked to successful post-16 courses such as the City and Guilds Institute's '365'.   With the emergence of such 'whole curriculum' courses for particular groups of pupils, the future for PSE work in integrating pupils of differing abilities looks bleak.

FUTURE POSSIBILITIES

We have seen that the last two years of mandatory schooling for the 'less academic' pupil may be on the point of undergoing radical changes   towards 'whole curriculum' courses [4].   We have also argued that these changes are similar in parts to some of the work which was done in the social and life skills areas of MSC sponsored post-16 schemes, and we drew attention to the growing association between social and lifeskills trainers and schools. Here we noted that their rapid successes within MSC had been with the 'disaffected', the 'less academic', those who had failed at school or whom school had failed.   Should such approaches be seen to be successful in providing an 'Education for Life' for 'less academic ' pupils, they will surely be accepted as the 'solution to the problem' which senior personnel in schools are searching for. Such a solution, the very success of such a solution building in PSE concerns across the curriculum, may distract us and others from the

commitment we outlined at the beginning of this
paper.
       The major source of the distraction is clear:
teachers of PSE have often insisted as we do,
that the methodology of PSE teaching is crucial.
Successful PSE work hinges on certain sorts of
relationships obtaining between teachers and pupils,
and pupils and pupils. These relationships mean
that the teacher cannot be viewed as the ever ready
source of knowledge and expertise. Such relationship
may be hindered by the trappings of the traditional
classroom, the layout of desks, the physical position
of the teacher, the way in which a board is used.
Many PSE teachers of our acquaintance are already
involved in the new 14-16 initiatives, where some are
finding that it is possible to build such relationshi
in a different environment for schooling. If, howeve
these changes are to take place more generally for on
the 'less academic', then what chance those commitments we started with in this paper?
       Briefly, we can sketch out some future scenarios
first, that all 14-16 year olds will experience PSE
but in differentiated programmes, which can fit, in
timetable terms, the nature of the routes pupils
are pursuing;   second, that PSE work will be phased
out for the 'academic' pupils from 14-16. The old
argument about these pupils not really needing it
could support this line of development, and, anyway
they may have experienced PSE in years 1,2 and 3.
       Both of these possibilities must be fought
against, for both seem to contradict the essence
of PSE. The 'hidden curriculum' message of both
is that, even within a comprehensive system, it is
proper that different groups of pupils should receive
a different and differentiated 'education for life'.
an education which stops pupils speaking to one
another, stops them relating to one another from
the age of 14.
       The third scenario is that time and space will
be given to PSE work which brings these groups
together, despite the difficulties of organisation,
particularly for staff who manage the timetable.
It will be necessary to live with the possibility
that this will create additional obstacles to
success with the 'less academic' pupils on their
'whole curriculum' routes. Our own pessimism as
to likely outcomes has probably been clear enough.
We do think that teachers who regard themselves as
PSE teachers, as well as any teachers with concern
for the personal and social development of 14-16 year
olds, will need to work hard for this third scenario.

However, we will conclude by noting that there is an
even more ambitious future possibility: one which
certain LEAs such as Manchester, with their long-
term aims for the 'Alternative Curriculum Strategies'
Project, and ILEA, with their 'Hargreaves Report',
have in mind. Of course, this scenario is dependent
on changes in the experience of schooling for all
4th and 5th years, leading to a worthwhile 'education
for life' for all pupils. One central plank in such
a programme would be a development of pupils' understandings of 'oneself and others': understandings
grounded in meetings, talk, and relationships between
pupils with different pasts and future in our society.

NOTES

    1. CCDU was founded in 1976, and funded
by eleven Yorkshire and Humberside LEAs with Leeds
University as the base. The Unit has developed a
distinctive training model consisting of a programme
of training teachers etc to train others in turn.
Various courses have been developed in counselling
skills, careers education, and lifeskills. The
current director, Barbara Pearce, has been heavily
involved in the development of 'Trainee Centred
Reviewing!'. Further information can be obtained
from: CCDU, University of Leeds, 22 Clarendon Place,
Leeds, LS2 9JT. Well known figures in the field who
have been involved in the development of the CCDU
include Barrie Hopson and Mike Scally, who founded
Lifeskills Association in 1978. Lifeskills associates is involved in counselling, training, and publishing, and operates in industrial, government and
educational systems in the UK and elsewhere.
    2. Kenneth David's Personal and Social Educa-
tion in Secondary Schools provides an excellent
overview of the area, as does the Further Education
Curriculum Review and Development Unit (FEU) in
Beyond Coping. Other useful sources are Hopson and
Scally's Lifeskills Teaching, Button's Group Tutoring
for the Form Tutor, McGuire, Priestley et al's
Social Skills and Personal Problem Solving and the
Active Tutorial work series.
    3. The project has been reported on in an
interesting way in the Times Educational Supplement
(27.1.84), and produces a regular Newsletter. Copies
of the latter and further information can be got via
the Project Director, Ethel Milroy, or Project Leader,
Mike Cockett, at 'Brook House', Hathersage Road,
Manchester M13 OJA.

4. At this point we would like to express our appreciation to Rob Halsall for his many helpful comments on this article, and in particular on the final section.

REFERENCES

Button, L. (1981) Group Tutoring for the Form Teacher, Hodder and Stoughton.

David, K. (1983) Personal and Social Education in Secondary Schools, Longman for Schools Council.

Davies, B. (1979) From Social Education to Social and Life Skills Training: In Whose Interests? National Youth Bureau.

Further Education Curriculum Review and Development Unit (1980) Beyond Coping: Some Approaches to Social Education, FEU.

Hustler, D. and Halsall, R (Eds) (1983). The Curriculum 14-16: An Education for Life? Manchester Polytechnic.

Hopson, B. and Scally, M. Lifeskills Teaching Programmes No.1. Lifeskills Associates, Leeds 1980.

Hopson, B. and Scally, M. Lifeskills Teaching Programmes No.2. Lifeskills Associates, Leeds 1982.

Hopson, B. and Scally, M. (1981) Lifeskills Teaching, McGraw Hill.

ILEA. (1984). Improving Secondary Schools (The Hargreaves Report).

Lancashire Education Authority, (1980,1981), Active Tutorial Work (Books 1-5), Blackwell.

Manpower Services Commission (1973), Instructional Guide to Social and Lifeskills Training.

Manchester LEA. (1980) A Curriculum for Today and Tomorrow.

Pearce, B. et al (1980) Trainee Centred Reviewing, CCDU.

Priestly, P., McGuire, J. et al (1978) Social Skills and Personal Problem Solving, Tavistock.

Times Educational Supplement, Finding a happy Medium, TES 27.1.84, p.8-9.

Chapter Five

MATHEMATICS COUNTS - BUT NOT FOR THE PUPILS

Ted Cuff

INTRODUCTION

'Why can Johnny not do arithmetic?' With this
question, Hans Freudenthal chose to open up and
focus his plenary address on Major Problems of
Mathematics Education at the Fourth International
Congress on Mathematical Education (ICME, 1983, p.2).
In answering his own question, he produced _inter alia_
several examples of his own success in sorting out
the problems of various children, a plan for the rethinking and re-structuring of teacher education and
the dismissal of the bulk of educational research
as irrelevant to practical teaching. In positive
terms, he advocated the need to learn to observe
learning processes which '....involves analysing,
by which I don't mean averaging or applying other
statistical procedures nor fitting the observational
data into preconceived patterns of developmental
psychology' (ICME, p.2).
    We like the clear and direct formulation of what
Freudenthal takes to be the major problem and, as
far as it goes, his candidate solution in terms of
developing a methodology which eschews the whole
paraphernalia of counting, measuring and producing
statistical generalisations in favour of one stressing the need to look at what goes on in the everyday
world, here the everyday world of the mathematics
classroom.
    We depart from him, however, in two ways. First,
both authors are non-mathematicians and therefore
have no vested professional interests in the organisation, development and expansion of the subject.
In fact, our 'vested interest' is in having been
on the receiving end of the efforts of mathematics
teachers who made little noticeable change in the
development (or otherwise) of our mathematical

knowledge. Consequently - and secondly - we feel we
have some awareness of and sensitivity to a major
problem of Mathematics Education which is noticeably
absent from Freudenthal's formulations: the fear
and anxiety which can result from 'mathematical
blockage'. Of course, it is possible that Freudenthal takes this problem as given, takes it for
granted as a ubiquitous feature of any mathematical
educator's existence. Certainly, he is not alone
in not making it explicit: in 722 double columned
pages produced by 300 or so authors of the Proceedir
of the Fourth International Congress of Mathematical
Education (ICME, 1983) direct references to fear and
anxiety are scarce (cf. p.14, p.656).

   Thus our formulation of the problem is not only
'why can Johnny not do arithmetic?', but also 'why
can the attempt to do arithmetic cause so much fear
and anxiety in Johnny?'

   Our standpoint in approaching this reformulated
problem is not only that of the non-mathematician,
though we would not wish to underplay its importance
We are also professional sociologists and educators
which affords us a certain angle of vision into the
area. What this sociological standpoint looks like
will become clearer later, but to avert for the
reader this identity immediately conjuring up
'background variables' like home, family and school
coming neatly together in an input/output analysis
and nicely encapsulated in several tables of statistical data, we reiterate our agreement with Freudenthal's emphasis on studying the learning processes
i.e. looking at what actually goes on in the world.

   In pursuing our problem, we intend to examine
how it has been treated in the recently published
report of the Committee of Enquiry into the Teaching
of Mathematics in Schools, Mathematics Counts
(Cockcroft, 1982) in view of the important - even
seminal - status such reports can be accorded. We
will also look more briefly at other published work,
noticeably an important study of maths panic and
anxiety (Buxton, 1981).

   We then go on to discuss how this work squares
with everyday classroom reality, key aspects of
which we try to recall by means of transcriptions
of tape-recorded classroom talk. Here we will see
that these materials reflect much else besides the
'learning processes' referred to by Freudenthal.

THE COCKCROFT REPORT

The Report concludes:

> ...The setting up of our Committee demons-
> trated a widespread view that action was
> needed in order to meet the perceived national
> need for a numerate population. During the
> past three years we have received many exp-
> ressions of support for our work which indic-
> ate a widespread belief that every boy and
> girl need to develop, whilst at school,
> an understanding of mathematics and con-
> fidence in its use. In our view this can
> only come about as the result of good mathe-
> matics teaching by teachers who have been
> trained for their work and who receive con-
> tinuing in-service support. It must there-
> fore be the task of all who share this belief
> to support and encourage the implementation of
> the changes which we believe to be necessary
> and to make it clear that, as part of the
> education which our children receive, mathe-
> matics counts.

> (Cockcroft, para 810)

This conclusion seeks to persuade: it is not
saying that mathematics counts, but that it should
be made to count. There is plenty to do to secure
this end and the appropriate measures are set out
in the document.
    Within a year the status of the Report had been
transformed, at least as far as the Department of
Education and Science was concerned. In 1983 a
free booklet was issued to all primary schools,
Cockcroft: an introduction for primary schools,
which had the following preamble:

> Mathematics counts, the report of the Cock-
> croft Committee of Inquiry into the teaching
> of mathematics in schools, is the most auth-
> oritative document about school mathematics
> to be published for many years. It contains
> much of importance for those who teach
> mathematics in primary schools. In a Par-
> liamentary statement the Secretary of State
> for Education and Science said that 'the
> report has set out an analysis of the
> purposes of mathematics education which

71

is striking in its realism and lucidity. It
has put forward recommendations which call
for early action by all involved..... Our
tasks is to build on the foundations which
the Cockcroft Committee has laid.' This is
a task in which each primary school needs
to take part.

This paper is an introduction to the report
for teachers in primary schools and sets
out some of the messages from the report
which are of particular relevance to those
who teach mathematics in the primary years.
The Cockcroft Committee has presented its
arguments and conclusions in a way which
makes them accessible to those who are not
mathematics specialists and this paper often
makes use of the words of the report itself.

This introduction is not, however, in any sense
a summary of the report nor a substitute for
it. It is, therefore, important that a copy
of Mathematics Counts should be available in
each primary school for teachers to consult.
It is important, too, that the head and at
least one member of staff should have a clear
view of the report as a whole so as to be
able to explain and interpret the relevant
sections to colleagues.

Copies were also sent to Institutions Providing
Initial Training for Primary School Teachers and
in a covering letter the booklet was referred to as
'a readily accessible aide-memoire to both staff
and students.....'. Thus Cockcroft seems destined
to become to mathematics teaching what A Language
for Life (Bullock,1975) was for language in schools,
nanely, the point of reference, arbiter, debating
ground for what to do in the teaching of the subject
Alternatively put, it provides a rhetoric of justification for what is done in schools by way of
changing approaches and methods to teaching, crit-
icising or reforming colleagues and developing and
organising appropriate in-service training courses -
all with a view to improving the teaching of mathematics, making mathematics count.
    What, then,is being advocated for improving
the teaching of mathematics in terms of aims,
content, methods and mechanisms?
    The aims or purposes of mathematics are set
out clearly. The subject is viewed primarily as a

concise unambiguous means of communication. It has utility in many fields including everyday life and it is inherently interesting, containing as it does appealing puzzles.

In terms of content, there is hardly any piece of mathematics that every adult uses, but everyone has some need to count, tell the time, weigh, measure, understand timetables, understand simple graphs and charts and to approximate and estimate mentally. The needs of employment and of Higher Education vary considerably. The primary school has the task of laying down basic foundations and some LEAs have issued guidelines of content. For Secondary Schools, the Report sets out a list of essentials, a foundation list of topics for all pupils.

This content involves facts and skills, conceptual structures and general strategies (choosing which skills to employ, strategies to adopt, knowledge to use) and requires teaching skills at all levels which include

- exposition by the teacher
- discussion (teacher- pupil, pupil-pupil)
- practical work
- consolidation and practice of fundamental skills and routines
- problem solving including application to everyday situations
- investigational work

Here we note the particular stress that is placed on discussion. The Report emphasises that discussion should go beyond short question and answer sequences during the teacher's expositions. Instead, there should be 'opportunities to talk about mathematics, to explain and discuss results which have been obtained, and to test hypotheses'. (para 246). Discussion is vital to establish links between topics. In the primary school 'Language plays an essential part in the formulation and expression of mathematical ideas' (para 306). Children hope to learn to recognise the same idea with different forms of words. Similarly, in secondary schools '...pupils should read and write and talk about mathematics in a wide variety of ways....at all stages pupils should be encouraged to discuss and justify the methods which they use' (para 458). We shall take up these references later when we examine some transcriptions of classroom talk.

Finally, we turn to mechanisms for implementing these changes. Of course, the main mechanism is the class teacher. Somehow the classic problem of educating the educator has to be overcome and class teachers have to adopt new approaches in the light of the redefinition/classification of the subject as set out in the Cockcroft Report. The teacher will be helped in this endeavour by a key person: the Maths Coordinator in a primary school, and the Head of Maths in a secondary school. These key persons therefore have prime responsibility for interpreting the Report in practical everyday terms. To assist them as well as ordinary teachers there will be in-service training courses at Teachers Centres or Institutions of Teacher Training. Further, teachers are encouraged to get together more, to see one another's work in different schools as well as en-gaging in systematic team work in the same school in formulating schemes of work and evaluating their workings.

Of course, the above is the barest sketch of just some of the arguments and recommendations of the Cockcroft Report. This report is 309 pages long and incorporates a very large number of statements, assertions, summaries of empirical research, illustrations and suggestions. We suggest, however, that just as no practising teacher could derive much idea of what to do in a classroom situation from our bare sketch, similarly no clear guidance can be derived from the full report for the opposite reason, i.e. there is simply too much materials to assimilate. Hence the need for a translator, or at least a translation - into the nitty-gritty of classroom interaction.

Now, the Report is not geared to classroom interaction. By emphasising discussion, by stressing the need for pupils to understand what they are doing when making computations, it alludes to inter-action. It does not, however, attempt to describe it or to take such realities fully into account. Rather, the Report is basically concerned with output; how to produce a numerate adult population, how to make mathematics count with the children in order to secure this important end. By definition, 'good' teaching together with the necessary re-sources and parental and other support - all as defined in the Report - can secure this end. In short, with a clearer sense of purpose, relevant contents, improved methods and suitable organisa-tional mechanisms, the seemingly perennial problems of mathematics teaching can be overcome.

This summary is not meant to imply that we or anyone else has tremendous faith in the practical outcomes of the Cockcroft Report. Everyone knows how
such Reports seek to 'cover the ground'. With the
usual wide and varied collection of persons com-
prising the Committee, compromise is inevitable and
the final product seldom greatly raises hopes or
induces great feelings of disappointment. After
all, it is only another report - this time on
Maths - and there are plenty more where they came
from.

MATHS PANIC, FEAR, and ANXIETY

Nevertheless, to those of us who have undergone the
anxiety induced by mathematical blockage, any
promise is good news, if not for ourselves at this
stage then at least for the younger generation.
Certainly, the Report is very clear on the difficulties of teaching maths and the troubles it can
cause for all concerned. As early as paragraph
11, these problems are touched on: the subject
is difficult because it is not used all the time,
unlike ordinary language; it does not come 'naturally', having to be learned and practised extensively; and mistakes make maths unintelligible,
in contrast to ordinary language. To do maths
requires confidence: it takes a lot of time and
many children need a great deal of help. Further,
commissioned research indicated:

> The extent to which the need to undertake
> even an apparently simple and straight-
> forward piece of mathematics could induce
> feelings of anxiety, helplessness, fear
> and even guilt in some of those interviewed
> was, perhaps, the most striking feature of
> the study. No connection was found between
> the extent to which those interviewed used
> mathematics and the level of their education-
> al qualifications; there were science grad-
> uates who claimed to use no arithmetic and
> others with no qualification who displayed
> a high level of arithmetical competence.
> Nor did there appear to be any connection
> between mathematical competence and occupa-
> tional grasp.....The feelings of guilt to
> which we referred earlier appeared to be
> especially marked among those whose academic
> qualifications were high and who, in conse-
> quence of this, felt that they 'ought' to

have a confident understanding of mathematics, even though this was not the case
(para 20, 21).

The Report also notes that even among persons who
can do some maths calculations they may lack
confidence because they do not use 'proper
methods'. There is a feeling that there is always
a 'proper' method. The reasons for failure and
consequent dislike of maths were various, e.g.
unsympathetic teacher, parental pressure, criticism
by other members of the family.
The notion of maths-induced anxiety is graphi-
cally illustrated in Buxton's Do You Panic about
Maths: Coping with Maths Anxiety. In our experience, Buxton is a rare bird: a mathematician who
has a real insight and feel for the pains and
troubles of non-mathematicians. He did not need
survey evidence to know that 'there is much evidence
that many adults greatly dislike maths. The feeling
of uncertainty and anxiety are constantly expressed
to me at parents' meetings at schools, and also in
many casual conversations. The statements about
their own bad experiences at school are often
explicit and well remembered' (Buxton, 1981, p.11).
He is quite clear that maths can be as much an
emotional as a rational business in view of the way
it can generate such fearful reactions. In his
view they could well derive from the maths teacher
being an authority figure, the pupil feeling that
speed of response is of the essence, the public
nature of such responses, i.e. the fear of some
sort of degradation in front of classmates, and
fear of the unknown. Regarding this last point,
he suggests 'There has, from the time of Pythagoras,
been a certain mystique about the subject, and this
is reflected in (the) view that this mountain is
peopled by those who do know about it and claim
what fun it all is' (p.9). As one of his respondents
says: 'I dislike doctors because they seem to have
wrapped themselves round in magic - mystique - and
I feel mathematicians have the same quality' (p.28).
Buxton tries to produce a theoretical explan-
ation of maths panic. In the time afforded by a
sabbatical year he explored the maths problems of
a sample of reasonably well educated adults ('O'level
and sometime 'A'level) by holding over 30 2-hour
meetings with a group of seven and over a dozen
interviews with each of three persons. Most of
his sample represent real horror stories in terms
of maths anxiety. For example, Elaine was formerly

a Head of a Girls' Grammar School and became a LEA Inspector. Although she enjoyed timetabling at school, she had traumas and lost sleep about her inability to do long division. In fact, she nicely illustrates the point in the Cockcroft Report about how reasonably well educated people can have the most anxiety.

Buxton is keen to de-mist the mystique. He feels it can be done if a different image of maths can emerge namely, the positive view as opposed to the negative view as set out below:

NEGATIVE VIEW OF MATHS	POSITIVE VIEW OF MATHS
1. Fixed, immutable, external, intractable, uncreative	Experiential, exploratory, creative
2. Abstract, unrelated to reality	Abstract at times but often directly related to the most practical problem
3. Mystique, accessible to a few	Open to all, but penetrated more by some people
4. Collection of rules, facts, to be remembered	Network of constant relationships, easily remembered when understood
5. Sometimes an affront to commonsense	Always recognisable with the internal logic of the mind
6. Time test	Contemplative, requiring concentration individual attention, never needing haste
7. Judgements made on personal worth, not only intellect	An area in which judgements of ability should carry no more weight than in other studies
8. Concerned largely with computation	About relationships in general

(from Buxton, Chapter 10)

With most of his sample, Buxton did manage to help
them overcome some of their maths anxiety. It is
not clear, however, that the theory be postulates
was the basis for his success. In it, he attempts
to create a model using Popper's notion of three
worlds (The External World, a person's own Mental
World, the World of Statements) in conjunction
with Skemp's theories of intelligence and goal-
directed activity. The consequence may be the
creation of another mystique to be demisted. We
do, however, find the notion of 'worlds' interesting in that he seems to advocate underplaying the
fashionable stress on making maths relevant to
the everyday world in favour of concentrating on
its cognitive nature. Basically, panic derives
from a disjunction between these worlds (Buxton's
'delta one' and 'delta two').

In fact, he is clearer though less theoretic-
ally ambitious whenever he turns to commenting on
the talk with his respondents and in suggesting
various pointers to create more security for them.
Thus he suggests designing questions which can
secure a high proportion of right answers, warns
against the dangers of overlong silences, stresses
the importance of treating answers with respect
and brings out the difficulty for students in being
able to pose well constructed questions, or to
explain why they do not understand something.

Buxton fills out in some detail the notion of
maths anxiety bringing out some of the attitudes,
values and conceptions of maths, which can generate
this emotional state. His feel for some of the
interpersonal relationships involved is also
excellent. What he cannot offer, however, is any
direct translation to the everyday problems of
the classroom. The work of translation has to be
done, just as with the Cockcroft Report, by practising teachers.

SOME CLASSROOM REALITIES

We now turn to our transcriptions as a way of trying
to see some of what actually goes on in maths classrooms. The transcripts are simply those that were
easily available: they are not any kind of 'sample'
but we feel that they are not untypical of teaching
currently going on. They number 11 in all, 5 infant, 4 junior and 2 secondary, covering ages 4-13,
and as they come to some 87 pages of script, it is
not possible to reproduce more than illustrative
excerpts here.

What we intend to do is to pull out the 'grossly observable features' that we, as non-mathematicians, can plainly see in them. Many of these features will be familiar to readers, but it is important to review them if we are to assess the advice in the Cockcroft Report and elsewhere in helping out with the problems of 'Why cannot Johnny do arithmetic?' and 'why can the attempt to do so cause so much fear and anxiety for him?'

Question-Answer sequences

Overwhelmingly in all types of schools the basic format of talk is Question and Answer (Q-A) where the teacher asks the questions, the pupil supplies (or not) the answer. This format is adopted in whole class, small group and individual situations. A typical example from a whole class situation in a primary school is:

Excerpt (i)

T: Right, tell you what, best thing is, turn your chairs right round, that's it. Come a bit closer. Just put Adam's chair there. Can you all see the blackboard clearly? Right. Smashing. No, the hedgehog will be alright there, for the moment. Now, over the last few weeks, we've been looking at different ways of showing numbers, haven't we?

P: Yes

T: What was the first thing we used?

P: Sticks and stones

T: Sticks and stones. What was the next thing we used?

P: String

T: String, what did we do with the string?

P: Tied knots in it.

T: Tied knots in it. Then what were the... what was the....what did we follow up with?

P: Um.... them blocks

T: Them blocks, what's...what are them blocks called?

P: Dienes

T: Dienes blocks, that's it. The important thing we were doing all the time was, organising our numbers into.....?

P. Sets

(From Transcript E)

79

And we see the same pattern in the second year of a secondary school:

Excerpt (ii)

T:	....What we're going to do is represent this on a pie-chart. What are we goin to do first?
Diane:	Draw a circle
T:	Draw a circle, radius 4 cm. What are we going to do now - Richard?
Richard:	Draw a radius
T:	Lee - what are we going to do now?
Lee:	Measure 10°
T:	How am I going to do that?
Lee:	With a protractor
T:	Measure off an angle of 50°. Doesn't matter which way you go. Come on, there's too much talking. You've got to concentrate. There's something I forgot to tell you. How could we tell if we'd made a mistake before we draw it?
Lee:	Times then all up
T:	Add them all up and see if they make 360°. If you need any help ask now. Put your hands up. I'm going to give your tests back while you do this. There are some more examples for you to do next. Would you like to give them out?

(From Transcript J)

The Distribution of Talk

In effect, the Q-A sequence is a two-party exchange, where the teacher is one party and the pupil con-stitutes the other. Just as in any other two-party conversation, there has to be a one-person-speaks-at-a-time rule to allow the talk to proceed in an orderly manner. Hence in the teacher's slot this ordering is secured with such devices as 'hands up' (see Excerpt (ii) above). She also has to use the slot for everything else, such as explaining issuing instructions. In fact, the major occasional departure from the ubiquitous question is the issue of an instruction, again well illustrated in Excerpt (ii).

Speaker selection

Given the Q-A structure and a distribution of talk
in which the teacher takes the initiative and produces the bulk of the talk, it is also true that
speaker selection also becomes her prerogative
Sometimes she selects the answerer, sometimes the
question is open to several so that class members
can self select to answer. Thus in Excerpt (i),
the class are self selecting, while in Excerpt (ii)
the teacher moves away from this mode to nominate
Richard, presumably because she felt he was inatten-
tive as his incorrect reply might bear out.

Remembering

Remembering what happened before, especially the
last time, is a recurrent theme. It brings out the
obvious point that lessons are not one-off but are
in a chain or sequence so that what can be done now
depends on what was done last. Excerpt (i) directly
invites the class to recall what has been happening
over the last few weeks. In Excerpt (ii), however,
the teacher is seeking to draw on earlier teaching.
The lesson newly introduces pie charts and draws on
previous knowledge of presenting information (bar
charts, pictograms) as indicated by:

    Excerpt (iii)

  T: What do you think a pie-chart is?
  C: It's a circle
  C: It's $360°$ at the middle....and you
       measure the degrees
  C: It's divided into sections, and it's the
       size to indicate a piece of information
  T: The size depends on the information we are
       given. Now, can anyone think very care-
       fully why we might want to use a pie-chart
       rather than a bar-chart or a picto-gram?
  C: No
  S: To show how many per cent there are
  T: Well, sort of percentage. I don't want
       you to go into details.....
  S: So you see how big it is....takes up the
       space....
  T: Sandra's on the right line....what I'm
       looking for. Pie-charts are used mainly
       for comparison. What I want you to do is
       put the heading 'Pie-charts' in your books.
  C: Which book Miss?

                    (From Transcript J)

Getting it right or wrong

Not being able to remember is one thing; not being able to do it is another. A ubiquitous product of the Q-A sequences is the nomination or self selectio of the answerer to get it right or wrong before an audience which can consist of just the teacher, the teacher plus another student or two, or the whole class. In Excerpt (ii), both Richard and Lee get the answer wrong. Richard's answer is ignored and Lee is invited to give the correct version. When Lee gets it wrong, the teacher amends the answer without underlining the point and carries on (i.e. Lee-Times them up- T Add them up). Thus, how baldly the answer comes off as success or failure depends to some extent on the skills of the teacher, but the rightness or wrongness is still clear to all Certainly, Nick's difficulties are for all to see in the next excerpt:

Excerpt (iv)

((Teacher at desk in primary school seeing individual children))

T:	Yes Nick
Nick:	....What is....that?
T:	What does 'it say'
T & Nick:	Six multiplied by
Nick:	Three
T:	What does multiplied mean?
Nick:	.....add some.....taken.....
T:	((to class in general)) What does multiplied mean
Class:	Times
T:	Again
Class:	Times
T:	Thank you

(From Transcript F)

The taken-for-granted nature of the right-wrong frame of reference for all parties comes over in the following excerpt where the pupils find the teacher has made a mistake, albeit a deliberate one:

Excerpt (v)

T: Its place...the place we put the number is very important isn't it. Once we put it

in that place, it stands for something
else. In this case it stands for units
and in this case it stands for tens,
and sometimes to help you you can put
hundreds, tens and units at the top of
a sum, can't you. Right, you've done lots
of adding up, but let's have a look at
just one, before we start, adding up some
hundreds, tens and units and try and
picture what we've been doing with the
Dienes blocks recently, alright. Let's ..
2 hundred and what, shall we have?

P: 65
T: 265, right, that's a good number
P: And...and, 194
T: 194...194...right
P: That's wrong
T: Sorry...
P: It's wrong
T: It's wrong...what's wrong
P: Cos you put um....the bottom numbers in
    the wrong place.
P: You put the hundreds in...
T: But I see that in children's books....
    children do that in books, that say, oh,
    that's it, that's the 2 numbers, I'll write
    them down
P: It's not
T: It's not?
P: You put the 1 underneath the 2
T: Then 1 underneath...
P: The 9 underneath the 6 and the 4 underneath
    the 5
T: Why is that
P: Because then you can add it up instead of
T: I can add it up like that....there you are,
    it's easy, 5 and 0, I can add it up like
    that
P: But that'll be wrong
T: Why is it going to be wrong?
P: Well you can't take 2 away from 9
T: We're not taking anything away...we're
    adding...oh sorry, I should have put that,
    we're adding these up
P: It's...the bottom number's in the wrong
    place
T: That's the word, it's this place all the
    time. The bottom number's in the wrong
    place. Everything there is in the wrong
    places. The 4, which is really 4...
P: tens....units

```
T:    Units...is in fact stuck in the...
P:    Tens
T:    Tens....the 9, which is really 9
P:    Tens
T:    Is stuck in the...
P:    Hundreds
T:    In the hundreds, and the 1 has suddenly
      become...
P:    Thousand
T:    A thousand, so that's no good.  So the
      first thing we've got to do is to get
      everything in the right place.  264 it
      was and 1 hundred
P:    No....5
T:    Was it, oh.  Wrong again...and one hundred
      and ninety.
```

(From Transcript E)

Listening

The nature of the classroom talk in our transcripts
is designed to require each pupil to listen as anyone
may be nominated by the teacher to take up the next
slot to answer a question at any time.   The teacher
too has to listen to what the pupils say though
there is not a great deal of listening to do given
the characteristics of the talk as described. It
is possible, however, for the right-wrong frame of
reference to shape the teacher's listening so
that she does not see the sense the pupil is making.
For example, the teacher produces a string of questions and cannot hear the pupil's answer as a correct
response to an earlier question:

   Excerpt (vi)

   T: Put your ten in the units column
            No no
            Come on Tricia
            You go to the units column and you
            take a ten
            Where do you put the ten. We put it
            in the.......units column don't we.
            Like we did there, and there, and
            there, and there, and there.
            Now how many units have you got there
            in the units column now?
   Tricia: Sixteen
   T: Do you know where they came from

Tricia	Tens.....and six
T:	Yes....and how many units in a ten?
	How many units in a ten?
	How many units in a ten?
Tricia:	Sixteen
T:	No

(From Transcript F)

Getting Through and Getting On

Teachers have the task of developing individual mathematical abilities for all members of their class. The transcripts clearly show the pressures induced by giving individual attention yet at the same time keeping the whole class going. What the teacher regards as an interruption in terms of teaching pupil A is, for pupil B, the interrupter his share of the teacher's attention and his treatment by her.

Excerpt (vii)

| Alex: | What shall I know what I've bought in there |
| T: | Oh you're on the same page as Madeleine. Would you like to work together with Alex. Thank you very much. Would you like to explain how you did that, and let him have a go, and see if he gets the same answer. |

(From Transcript H)

Here the teacher manages the interruption and gets on with teaching another pupil by asking Alexander to work with Madeleine, thereby ostensibly using the technique of pupil teaching pupil. As this device is unusual in the transcript, we may enquire how much of a management rather than a pedagogic device it is here.

In this particular organisational arrangement, the teacher is sitting at her desk and seeing one child at the time and keeping the other going. The above excerpt illustrates one method of getting on. In whole class situations, the theme of getting on, getting through the work is obviously managed differently. We saw in, for example, Excerpt (ii), how 'wrong' answers are ignored, pending the proferring of a correct one.

85

Individual and Cohort

It is perhaps worth bringing out as a separate
'grossly observable feature' of our transcripts
the way that an indispensable technique for teachers
is to treat an individual response as representing
the response of the whole class or cohort (cf Payne,
1980). Though teachers are charged with giving
everyone individual attention, they must perforce
use such techniques if they are to get through their
lesson plan, work scheme and syllabus. It is plainly
not possible in class-teaching situations to check
out everyone. Thus in Excerpts (i) and (ii) above
the one or two pupil answerers have to be taken
as speaking on behalf of the whole class.

Ordinary Language

It is also grossly apparent that the kind of language
used in the classroom talk throughout the 4-13 age
span covered by our transcripts is 'ordinary',
whether used by the teacher or by the pupils. Althoug
there are labels which are not too frequently encountered every day, e.g. equilateral triangles, or
not at all, e.g. number bases, there is little evidence that the talk reflects or neutrally describes
the kind of symbolic systems which are presumed to
characterise mathematics as a subject. Yet there
is evidence that there is something there to be
translated when the opportunity occurs.

CLASSROOM REALITIES AND THE PROBLEM OF UNDERSTANDING

In comparing our grossly observable features of
classroom interaction with the discussion of maths
in teaching to be found in the Cockcroft Report,
we can accept gratefully the notion of 'multiple
realities' found in Schutz (1973). For the world
of theorising about how maths should be taught,
even the world of maths itself, seems a long way
removed from the everyday setting of the maths
classroom.
        In essence, the concept of multiple realities,
as conceived by Schutz, brings out the fact that we
all operate in a number of different realities or
worlds. The notion of 'world' is not intended to
indicate physical or spatial separation; we all
live in one and the same world, but what this
world means to us is highly dependent on the
nature of our involvement which shapes our relevances
Simply put, what counts as important when we are

teaching a class is not the same as what counts
when we are on a committee talking about how classes
should be taught. In the class, we are in the
'world' of everyday life; in the committee we are
much nearer to a world of theorising about it; and
when operating as a subject specialist, as a mathematician, we have moved even further away from the
relevances of classroom teaching in favour of what
is required to operate as a good mathematician.

King (1982) explores this concept of multiple
realities in the context of the infant classroom.
He nicely shows how the children can and do enter a
number of different 'worlds' or orders of reality.
They can discuss what counts in these different
provinces of meaning. As he puts it:

> Children learn to share their teacher's
> definition of the nature of these provinces
> of meaning by reproducing them in their
> reading aloud, in their writing, in doing
> sums or problems and in painting and drawing.
> They also learnt which of these worlds they
> inhabited at the given time. Pink elephants
> may exist in one of the story worlds or the
> world of Mathematics, but never in the 'real'
> life world of news or of Peter and Jane or in
> a 'proper' painting.

> (King, 1982, p.245).

He also says that we need to know more about how
children enter these worlds of meanings and brings
out the point that the world of mathematics seems to
teachers more esoteric than other 'worlds'. Pupils
too needed some considerable shift of attention to
convert everyday life into mathematical realities,
e.g. turning heights into histograms or objects
into numbers.

Thus the concept of multiple realities might
serve to highlight a major way of grasping the
nature of the difficulties of many in doing mathematics, and the fear and anxiety which can be
generated by the attempt to understand that is
happening in maths lessons. The shift from a world
of pink elephants to one of real (grey) ones seems
far less radical than that of pink elephants to
their symbolic representation. If teachers regard
the world of mathematics as esoteric, we might
expect this view to be reflected in their teaching
and hence in their pupils. Other sources (e.g.
Quadling and Shuard, 1980) confirm this basic

uncertainty particularly among primary teachers,
most of whom have little specialism in mathematics,
<u>per se</u>. It is perhaps this distance between 'worlds
that underlies the 'mystique' referred to in our
earlier discussion and the reliance on experts
'out there' to provide the necessary teaching
materials (King, 1982, p.243). Certainly, given
these uncertainties, teachers are likely to welcome
the guidance of the Cockcroft Report to the extent
it can be converted into more meaningful everyday
classroom practices. The key word, however, is
'meaningful', for without an improvement in understanding, the Report will become yet another source of
outside authority.

Leaving on one side the teacher's feelings about
her own understanding of the world of mathematics,
we presume that she wants her pupils to be able to
move between that everyday world of the classroom
and the world of mathematics with the same amount of
comfort and confidence as between, say, one of the
worlds created in story time and the everyday world.
In short, to understand not only what is going on in
the world of mathematics and to appreciate that it
has a life of its own, but also to find that it can
and does link with the everyday world.
That is to say, it can be applied to the everyday
world to solve problems, but it is also intrinsic,
having game-like properties which operate in symbolic
systems. Cockcroft especially stresses the inherent
interest of Mathematics (para 12).

Now we appreciate that these references to the
'world of mathematics', 'symbolic systems' and so
on can seem somewhat theoretical in relation to the
excerpts of clasroom talk we produced in the discussion of classroom realities. In fact, it is
just this sort of gap or disjuncture that faces
the teacher in the classroom situation. She has to
gauge the nature of the pupils' understanding from
their verbal and written products. Our transcripts
in general - illustrated in the few excerpts we have
reproduced - might indicate what a challenging task
the teacher has in this respect. There are many
textbooks, reports and opinions regarding what
teachers might do or even what they ought to do.
What empirical investigation provides, such as that
afforded by the detailed examination of transcripts,
is the opportunity to see what the practical management of the classroom looks like. We can examine the
pupils' verbal productions, as heard by the teacher,
to see what they make of them in the cut-and-thrust
of classroom activity.

Here we focus in particular on the nature of the pupils' mathematical understanding. Our question is: in terms of actual classroom practices, how does understanding come about?

This is not simply our question, it is any teacher's question. From our transcripts, it seems a particularly difficult question for the maths teacher given the materials she has to work from in respect of pupils' verbal productions. Cockcroft advocates the greater development of oral work and discussion in maths, but given its symbolic nature and out-of-the-ordinary vocabulary, problems of doing so are great. This point is reinforced when note is taken of such detailed and painstaking work as Shuard and Rothery (1984) to bring out the difficulties and ambiguities of the sort of language used in maths textbooks. In fact we have noted, oral work is not so much discussion as finding answers - and short answers - to teacher's questions.

Inevitably, in order to gauge understanding the teacher has to make inferences about what the pupils' products 'really' mean. 'Correct' answers are not satisfactory if they do not display 'genuine' understanding: guessing, parroting, mimicking, are all no use. Thus much of the teacher's work is in testing out, checking out understanding. In Excerpt (v) the teacher in a whole class situation appears to do so with a deliberate 'mistake'. In a primary situation, those pupils who produce right answers to written questions are asked to do more examples to consolidate their understanding as in:

Excerpt (viii)

P: Mrs Smith
T: Yes that's right. Now do this one again
P: ....and this one
T: Well that's right but that's wrong
P: Yes

(From Transcript F)

Or in the case of a primary class where the teacher feels progress is being made, we have the following exchange:

(Excerpt (ix)

T: Shall I put that there? Who thinks I should put that there? Who doesn't think I should put that there? Well, I mean, you can, but if I was to ask you to write

> down 99.....in your books...just write
> down 99, you wouldn't write down 099,
> would you?
>
> P: No
>
> T: You would just write the 99, wouldn't you
> So we don't really need to put that there
> 1 take away 1 leaves you with an empty
> space so we might as well leave an empty
> space, okay? One more I want to look at
> before I give you some little ones to
> practice on yourselves, and they're not
> easy, beware. I've made them especially
> tough.
>
> P: Oh
>
> T: Because I know how clever you lot are.
> Let's try this one. This is a nasty one.
> that's a nasty one
>
> P: It's not, it's an easy one
>
> P: Easy
>
> T: Oh! Sally, shh...face the front and watch
> Sally.
>
> P: You take 100 away from the 200 and you
> put it on the tens, then you can take
> ten away. you can borrow ten from there.

(From Transcript E)

The point about teachers having to infer what pupils
verbal products can possibly mean in terms of understanding is posed sharply when we look at transactions with the whole class. We've already pointed
out the obvious fact that an individual's answer has
to stand for the reply of the whole class or cohort.
It is clearly not practical to ask each child to
answer. When teachers ask the whole class if they
have understood; the chorus of 'yes' or looks of
'bright attention' can be as much a social or sur-
viving response as one reflecting understanding.
To check out an individual pupil's understanding
requires him at least to proffer some sort of substantive answer. If it is wrong, then the analysis
of the reason requires painstaking effort on an
individual basis as Excerpt (vi) illustrates. We
have also noted, e.g. in Excerpt (ii), how a teacher
might simply ignore an incorrect response in order to
keep moving.

For the same practical reason - some progress
has to be made, some ground has to be covered - she
may supply the answer to her own question:

Excerpt (x)

T: Has that shape been halved?
P: Yes
T: No it hasn't. It's been cut in two,
     but it hasn't been halved, why?

(From Transcript F)

Or she may repair or fill out an 'incomplete' answer
as in the following interaction between a teacher and
a child, F:

Excerpt (xi)

T: Right. Will you give me a quarter of that
     apple, please?
F: Yes
T: Thank you. How much have you given me?
     A quarter or one .....
F: One apple
T: One piece of the apple
F: One piece
T: Give me another quarter
T: How many quarters have you given me?
F: .....one piece
T: You haven't given me one piece. How many
     pieces have you given me?
F: Two
T: Two pieces or two......?
F: ....quarters
T: That's right! Two quarters. Give me
     another quarter, please. So how many
     quarters have I got now?
F: Three quarters
T: Good girl. So give me another piece.
     And how many pieces have I got now?
F: Four quarters
T: Four quarters. Instead of four quarters
     what could I say? I've got one.....?
F: Apple
T: One whole apple. I'm going to give you
     some pieces now. I've got how many pieces
     altogether?
F: Four
T: Four pieces. I'm going to give you - that
     much. How much have you got?
F: Two pieces
T: Two pieces or two.....?
F: Halves
T: Oh.....come on!

91

F: Quarters
T: That's right. Two quarters. I've given you three pieces now....you've got.
F: I've got three quarters
T: That's right! And I take two away. What are you left with?
F: One quarter
   One quarter. So, if I cut something into quarters how many pieces will I get?
F: Four
T: Four. Shall we try it with a piece of paper?

(From Transcript G)

We note that both Excerpts (x) and (xi) concern the interaction of a teacher and a single pupil rather than the teacher addressing the whole class. In each the teacher seems to be trying to get the child to 'see' the answer. If we focus on Excerpt (xi) she eventually manages to secure the answer she is seeking, but then she straightaway embarks on a replication of the exercise in terms of using a piece of paper rather than an apple, partly t check out if the understanding is genuine, if the child has really 'seen' it, 'grasped' it. Presumably the sheer effort in securing a right answer raises such doubts. Equally, however, the sheer effort, the number of questions, the wholesale opportunities for the child to give the wrong (as well as the right) answer might be doing something to the child in terms of pressure and generating a state of anxiety. We stress this inference is ours, not the teacher's, for her interaction with this child occupies some 17 pages of transcript, involving something like 200 Question-Answer sequences. In other contexts, this pattern of interaction might be described as 'third degree' or even 'brainwashing'.

Certainly, the teacher here is inferring that this child is in difficulties and needs a lot of attention. In Excerpt (vi) we came across a broadly similar situation with 'Tricia'. In this case, we are fortunate in being able to draw on the expert analysis of a mathematical educator, Hilary Shuard, who has extracted from the whole transcript F the exchanges between the teacher and Tricia in a second year junior class and subjects them to detailed analysis. Tricia's problem concerns subtraction with exchange (35 minus 9) and Excerpt (vi) comes mid-way through the exchange.

Shuard starts with the basic premise that the child's utterances, responses, make sense. Hence when the teacher infers that Tricia's 'sixteen' in the penultimate utterance is wrong, she hears it that way because she assumes it was an answer to her last question, whereas it can be heard as a correct response to an earlier question. So the teacher is exasperated in seeing that the child does not even know how many units there are in a ten, but she does not take into account the possibility that Tricia is 'hanging on' to her own previous correct answer. Tricia may be unaware that the teacher has not been convinced that the earlier 'sixteen' demonstrated understanding. Consequently, she will also not be aware that the teacher has changed back, taking a few steps back to build up a 'sounder basis' for the answer 'sixteen'. In the next part of the exchange (not produced here) the teacher goes on to borrow unifix to tackle the problem of Tricia's understanding (or, rather, perceived lack of it) from yet another angle.

What the teacher is taking for granted is that the child is operating with the same sort of conversational competence that she herself routinely uses. As has been fully demonstrated (e.g. Sacks, et al. 1974) the teacher can standardly expect that answers do routinely follow questions and, also routinely, answers occur in the conversational slot immediately following the question. This conversational order, however, can be subverted by strings of questions such as we have in Excerpt (vi). Moreover, by this stage, there is obvious pressure on Tricia to find the right answer in a somewhat fraught situation as the teacher cannot refrain from showing some emotion. (' No, no, come on Tricia, no').

By the end of the intensive exchange, Tricia does produce the 'right' answer, '26', but only after she has used unifix to give the answer 'eight' to the question of 35 minus 26. Here we largely agree with Shuard's own inference that it would not be surprising if she tried random numbers in desperation at this stage of a rather abstract lesson.

We can only 'largely' agree because as non-mathematicians we are in no position to make judgements about the mathematical content of the lesson, its 'abstract' nature and so on. We also note that the professional Mathematics Educators do have a lot of faith in content, assuming that if only the content is right, a lot of problems will go away. The Cockcroft Report and the 4th International Congress

(ICME, 1983) amply reflect this view. It was this sort of faith which vested such hope in the New Mathematics, now virtually dismissed as a panacea and its content absorbed into the new 'mix' recommended in the Cockcroft Report.

What we can and have examined are some of the methods used to make inferences about the pupil's understanding of what was going on. As we see it, the teacher is using a model of mathematics content as a basis for generating a sequence of questions which imply a step-by-step progress to a correct answer. At each step, the pupil has to produce a correct mini-answer to a mini-question, until the jackpot question comes up and the problem is solved. From a child's viewpoint, the tactics probably overwhelm the strategy; each mini-question ('do you know where they came from', 'how many units in ten' etc etc) may well be <u>the</u> question, rather than a step on the way to somewhere. If true, this point makes so very important Shuard's 'hearer's preference of assuming the pupil makes sense.

As we have seen from our excerpts, however, the teacher has such a major role as a talker - mainly a giver of instructions and asker of questions - that notions of 'hearer's preferences' might sound a little odd. To be able to make inferences about the nature of a child's understanding, listening to the child, hearing what is said, is an obvious necessity. It is by no means something that is automatically done. What Excerpts (vi) and (xi) therefore illustrate is that problem of understanding and teaching are not necessarily overcome by breaking down class situations into individual encounters. What goes on in such interactions might prove to be more anxiety - provoking then anything that goes on in the comparative safety of the whole class. If we recall Buxton and the relevant parts of the Cockcroft Report, once such anxiety builds up the basis for confidence and progress can be destroyed. A vicious circle can be created viz. the poorer the understanding, the more attention the child is given, the greater the anxiety, panic, and so on.

Obviously, anxiety can derive fron not knowing what 'it's about', 'where we are going'. We have just examined a teacher's strategy in trying to get over a basic skill to Tricia (and the same point is also well illustrated in Excerpt (xi)) and how the teacher's immediate goals may not be apparent to the pupil. From the pupil's viewpoint, the trick might be to produce a correct answer to the question, but there are an awful lot of questions

94

it is difficult to keep up with them. The key
question, the exercise, finding the answer to
35 minus 9, may well be lost. This problem is
compounded when we realise that this answer is
simply one more step in working one skill.
There are plenty of others and they have to be
related if the child is to have a genuine understanding of mathematics. Such a goal is part of the
teacher's overall strategy: the pupil can merely
follow, step by step, where at each step the
'trick' is learned, the rule grasped.

From the teacher's standpoint, she has to
gauge when the rule has been grasped, when the
next step can be taken. If there are misunder-
standings what kind are they? Are they the kind
which can be remedied by a little more practice?
Are they the kind requiring some relearning of
steps already covered? Are they the kind generated
by the hopelessness of utter confusion? These
questions are answered on the spot at local level
without recourse to such high level theoretical
analyses of performance advocated, for example,
by Resnick and Ford (1981, p.67ff) which includes
examination of reaction time, hypothetical models
of learning and protocol analysis.

The teacher has to produce her own categor-
isation of types of mistakes (and, before long, of
pupils) and devise appropriate courses of action to
cope with them. The easiest recourse is to fault
the pupils - what's wrong with them, their IQ. It
is more challenging to ask what is wrong with the
teaching on the assumption that if the teaching is
right, the learning will ensue. Even the latter
approach may not be fruitful without some analytical
purchase on the nature of the problem.

CONCLUSION

We are suggesting that an important way of answering
our initial question, 'Why can Johnny not do arithmetic?' is to focus on actual classroom practices.
Here we emphasise the importance of examining what
actually goes on rather than what teachers and others
say goes on. As Garfinkel and Sacks (1970) point
out, such after-the-event 'glosses' are inevitably
reconstructions. These are recipient-designed for
particular hearers and are unlikely to recapture
the details needed to reconstruct the move-by-
move nature of classroom practices. For example,
if Tricia's teacher were to explain to colleagues

what she has been doing, a gloss or characterisation might involve talking about teaching 'subtraction with exchange' and the difficulties of so doing, perhaps because Tricia is 'slow'. The seen-but-unnoticed device of cumulating Q-A sequences and the effect such a practice might have in terms of the pupil's wider comprehension is likely to be glossed over. Naturally, much such talk is to do with sharing of feelings, generating mutual support and sympathy, rather than analysing performance in fine detail.

The methodology of using transcripts to examine classroom practices is not new (cf for example Adelman (1981), Woods and Hammersley (1977), Payne and Cuff (1982, 1983). Nevertheless, it still needs stimulating and encouraging as something teachers can do in order to develop a practical and relatively accessible means to look at their own actual practices, rather than to swop characterisations and anecdotes. Material help is needed to help to overcome the limitations on analysis often imposed by the perceived need to maintain a proper professional front with one's colleagues.

In examining our transcripts, to uncover their 'grossly observable features', we described quite a long list. Most of these features are characteristi of other types of lesson and are standard 'classroom realities'. One major difference is in terms o what counts as an answer to a question. In these transcripts, there is a very strong sense that there is only one 'right answer'. Another difference - not unconnected - is the focussed nature of the talk in terms of topic and the consequent limited scope for pupils to be able to contribute anything substantively. Although they also ask questions as well as supply 'candidate' answers, the questions are usually organisational not subject specific, e.g. 'Shall we need this box or shall I take it back' (Transcript H), This structure probably reflects what has been noted as the 'esoteric' nature of the subject, or, more bluntly, it is a hard subject.

Thus a major reason for maths anxiety may well be the difficulty of the subject. After all, we do not pose the question 'Why can Johnny not play the violin?' and exert every sinew to make playing the violin an end for everyone in compulsory schooling. In addressing the difficulty of the subject, the Cockcroft Report makes every effort to streamline it, to cut it back to bare essentials, to define an absolute minimum for the lowest level achievers in ordinary schools. The focus on maths anxiety, however, is only one of many concerns in what what is after all a comprehensive report aimed at the full range of ability, the need to produce mathematical high-fliers and the importance of incorporating new developments and technology. Thus the Report helps to clarify matters, especially in terms of content, but as we have pointed out, the how-to-doit question is left to the Report's interpretation and, basically, the teachers themselves. Most of these 'interpreters' are to be found in the Institutions of Teacher Training. The problem for them is how to avoid 'telling how' and to engage in 'showing how' where many of the audience may not be the teachers with the greatest problems. Another really big problem here is that of 'ironic' comparison: faulting teachers' recollections or reconstructions of their actual practices with counter-glosses of what better practices should look like. The trouble with ideals of better practices is that they usually occur in a hypothetically ideal world. We have refrained from describing the question of ironic comparison in terms of the 'theory-practice' dilemma, because all too often it comes off as school versus Teacher Training Institution. Whereas in fact, every teacher is a theoretician in terms of being able to describe their practice and to explain, rationalise, justify what they are up to in class. What we are after is the grounding of theories in strong data, whether or not they derive from teachers or teacher educators. What do these teacher theories look like in relation to the verbal transactions going on in actual classrooms?

In short, there are no easy, no cheap solutions to the problems of maths teaching and maths anxiety. There is a need, however, to find practical ways forward. One such way is the detailed analysis of classroom transactions by teachers themselves. If the Cockcroft Report succeeds in establishing for teachers the need for a thorough scrutiny of their own Mathematics teaching, then the scrutiny of their actual practices as reflected in recordings and transcribed materials is one way forward.

It is a practical way forward in a number of respects. First, it brings to the fore the fact that clearly emerges from our analysis of the oral nature of mathematical education. By and large, teachers do not expect their pupils in the 4-13 age range we have been considering to work from books in order to derive basic understandings of the subject, though, of course, books are used to provide exercises to do. Instead, the subject is

mediated through talk; there is an oral tradition
which is largely unexplicated and unexamined as
such. Its interactional workings are overlooked in
favour of the production of successful/unsuccessful
cognitive outputs, which, at their crudest, are
right or wrong answers. We hope to have emphasised
how important it is to scrutinise the talk and thereb
the process whereby such answers are produced. The
Cockcroft advocacy of more 'discussion' in maths
lessons is no more than lip service, a panacea, if
we are unaware of the structure and organisation and
working of this oral tradition.

Secondly, within this oral tradition of mathematical education, maths panic and anxiety are somehow generated for some pupils. No one knows very
much about why or how it happens. Many of the explanations are of a psychological kind, referring to the
way various stimuli might affect individual dispositions. Yet we know little about why some individuals 'see it', grasp 'the trick' and others do not.
We know little about why slightly varying repetitions
via examples may 'click' with some pupils, but
generate panic in others. In our discussion, we have
seen some cases which might be seedbeds for growing
anxiety and panic in terms of the understandings
being displayed by both teachers and pupils. We
have examined some kinds of misunderstanding, but have
only scratched at the problem with our few transcript
and excerpts.

Thirdly, by encouraging teachers to examine in
detail their own practices, their own embodiment of
this oral tradition displayed in their own verbal
transactions with their pupils, we can focus on the
here-and-now, rather than on recollections, the memory
work of retrospection. Although Buxton served us
well in bringing out the problem of maths panic and
anxiety, in his work he relied on ancient memories
from adults who had long left school. Whereas the
ordinary life of the classroom is routinely producing
vast quantities of 'up-to-date' materials everyday
in every school. After all, twenty four hours
spent in the everyday world of Ancient Rome would be
worth a life time of archaeological research.

ACKNOWLEDGEMENTS

I am very grateful to Derek Woodrow and Frank
Whitehead for bibliographical help, to Derek
Woodrow, again, Lilian Street and Hilary Shuard for
letting me use transcripts of maths lessons in their
possession, and to Wes Sharrock for discussions on
some of them.

I have also used some as yet unpublished analyses
of sections of her own transcripts by Hilary
Shuard of which 'Tricia's struggles' is the example
cited extensively. Of course, I am solely responsible for what has been done here with all this help.

REFERENCES

Adelman, C. (ed) (1981) Uttering, Muttering:
    Collecting, Using and Reporting Talk for
    Social and Educational Research, Grant McIntyre.
Buxton, L. (1981) Do you panic about Maths? Coping
    with Maths Anxiety, Heinemann Educational
    Books.
Cockcroft Report (1982) Mathematics Counts. Report
    of the Committee of Inquiry into the Teaching
    of Mathematics in Schools under the Chairmanship
    of Dr W.H. Cockcroft, HMSO.
D.E.S. (1983) Cockcroft: An Introduction for Primary
    Schools.
Garfinkel, H. and Sacks, H. (1970) 'On Formal Struc-
    tures of Practical Actions' in J.C. McKinney
    and E.A. Tiryakian (eds), Theoretical Sociology:
    Perspectives and Development, Appleton-Century
    Crofts, USA.
ICME (1983) Proceedings of the Fourth International
    Congress on Mathematical Education, Zweng, M.
    et al (eds), Birkhauser, Boston, USA.
King, R. (1982)'Multiple Realities and their Repro-
    duction in Infant Classrooms' in Richards, C.
    (ed) New Directions in Primary Education, The
    Falmer Press.
Payne, G.C.F.and Cuff, E.C. (1982) Doing Teaching:
    The Practical Management of Classrooms, Batsford.
Payne, G.C.F. and Cuff, E.C. (1983) Talk and More
    Talk: Studies in Classroom Interaction,
    Manchester Polytechnic.
Payne, G.C.F. and Hustler, D.E. (1980) 'Teaching the
    Class: the Practical Management of a Cohort',
    British Journal of Sociology, Vol 1, pp.49-66.
Resnick, L.B. and Ford, W.F. (1981) The Psychology
    of Mathematics for Instruction, Lawrence
    Erlbaum Associates.

Sacks, H, Schegloff, E, and Jefferson, G, (1974)
    'A Simplest Systematics for the Organization
    of Turn Taking for Conversation', in Schenkein,
    J. (ed), Studies in the Organization of
    Conversational Interaction (1978), Academic
    Press.
Schutz, A. (1973), 'On Multiple Realities' in
    Collected Papers, The problem of Social
    Reality ed M. Natanson, Martinus Nijhof,
    The Hague.
Shuard, Hilary and Quadling, D. (eds) (1980)
    Teachers of Mathematics: Some Aspects of
    Professional Life, Harper and Row.
Shuard, Hilary and Rothery, A. (eds) (1984) Children
    Reading Mathematics, John Murray.
Woods, P, and Hammersley, M. (eds) (1977) School
    Experience: Explorations in the Sociology
    of Education, Croom Helm.

ISSUES AND METHODS

The three contributions in this section look at
three issues: methods in the teaching of mixed
ability groupings in the secondary school; the
organisation of curriculum decision making; and
a radical reappraisal of methods of teaching
literacy skills for infant children.

John Evans and Brian Davies examine in some
detail the ever perplexing problems of change,
teaching and control of mixed ability groupings
as exemplified by an empirical case study of
Integrated Studies.

They argue that teaching mixed ability groups
is generally recognised as notoriously difficult.
When confronted with the task of catering for the
learning needs of a mixed ability group of pupils
many teachers respond by individuating their curriculum and method of teaching. That is to say,
they transpose the content of their curriculum to
work sheets from which pupils are then expected to
work largely independently of the teacher. Their
chapter focuses on the problems experienced by
teachers of Integrated Studies, when trying to
implement and work within an individuated curriculum
and on the problems faced by pupils trying to learn
and succeed within such a scheme which makes heavy
use of a worksheet approach.

On the basis of empirical evidence - observation,
recording classroom talk and the illustrative use of
transcripts - the authors argue that despite changes
in the surface appearance of teaching, the opportunities for learning and success which this approach
makes available to many pupils can remain very
limited indeed.

They identify a range of factors, some of which
limit, others facilitate the actions of teachers and
pupils alike. Despite individuation, teachers remain

in a position of having to secure the transmission of subject content to pupils within narrow time constraints. They demonstrate the impact of constraints of time and also content upon a teacher's action. In particular, they focus upon the form and content of classroom discourse, and on how the teacher uses the time available. The evidence suggests that the constraints of syllabus and pedagogy can promote a uniformity and patterning of teacher style in the integrated scheme throughout a department.

In addition to drawing attention to general features of teaching within the scheme, they also identify important, if subtle, differences in approach amongst teachers. In this context, the successful teacher, as seen by pupils, is neither 'radically' inspired, i.e. not attempting to step outside the structures of the course and generate 'new' knowledge nor overly 'autocratic', i.e. able to impose the course in its existing form upon pupils. Rather, his 'liberal' endeavours permit pupils a degree of 'working within' the limits and constraints on ability imposed by the worksheets generated out of the course organisation and structure. The authors suggest that pupil deviancy and alienation often stem not from a confrontation with 'reified' knowledge, but from pupil problems of access to it. They show that the requirements of pupil learning also correspond to the complex criteria which pupils use to assess teachers as 'good' or 'bad'. Hence the good teacher performs in such a way as to provide 'help' and understanding of content. His control is 'fair' and 'strict'. His humour also needs to be sufficient to break much of the routine and boredom associated with worksheet learning.

They conclude by arguing that new curricula and new modes of teaching do not necessarily bring about the desired effect of increasing sensitivity to, and greater achievement, with pupils of mixed ability. For such an outcome, teachers need to develop more than a 'reskilling' in terms of classroom control and management techniques. For, more basically, they have to develop an as yet unrealised better understanding of modes of transmission of knowledge in the classroom. Otherwise new methods can bring about old outcomes.

The other two contributions in this section both look at younger children, but both have a similar focus on differences of method and approach.

Carol Cummings critically examines her own practices as an infant teacher. She suggests that

teaching involves making decisions and deciding
what to teach comes under the heading of curriculum
decisions. In her chapter, she explores some aspects
of the relationship between curriculum decisions and
classroom teaching. From discussions of curriculum
planning it is often all too easy to get the impression that deciding what is to be taught is carefully planned outside the classroom and then imple-
mented. Thus individual teachers are seen to
formulate lesson plans in their heads even if not
on paper, while we know that for student teachers,
written lesson plans are usually seen as essential.
However, the relationship between what it is intended
the pupils should learn as an outcome of this
planning and what curriculum content they actually
come into contact with in a lesson is contingent:
it is dependent on the situated management of each
and every lesson.

Lesson and curriculum planning in itself does
not get the lesson taught. The activity of teaching
a lesson is inextricably embedded in the range of
decisions any teacher has to address when actually
handling a collection of pupils. In this chapter,
the author explores the dilemmas built into her own
and into every teacher's practice in these respects.
She displays the reality for her teaching of dilemmas
such as group versus individual learning, or pupil
discovery versus teacher didacticism. In the context of her infant classroom, these problems are
highlighted in the making of curricular decisions
concerning 'schemes' or 'themes'. Although in itself scheme work is not without its problems, the
challenge of theme work is even greater as the
teacher must perforce loosen or abandon the framework of organisation and follow the children's
interests. As Carol Cummings shows, however, in
reality the teacher does not and cannot abdicate
from guiding and shaping up the work, but control
is more delicate and surprises more likely. The
problems of opening up the organisation of the infant
day are highlighted by the frank expression and exploration of her doubts and anxieties in the light
of her own training and expectations, even though
she is an experienced teacher. This point is
compounded by a Postscript written some time later
from the vantage point of another post in another
school. Looking back, the opportunities in the
previous post seemed boundless in relation to this
new setting. Before, the shared understandings and
mutual expectations were simply taken-for-granted.
In the new school, they have still to be generated.

Only now are those features perceived to be pre-requisites for the more open-ended sort of curriculum decision making she once enjoyed.

A major advantage of this kind of theme work is in improving the quality of interaction between teachers and child. Perforce, the teacher must try to share in the child's way of viewing and understanding the world. This same point also underpins Nigel Hall's examination of teaching literacy skills to young children. He argues that despite differences in approach and technique, the methodologies of teaching children to read and write show many fundamental similarities. In particular they share modes of conceiving literacy as an activity which has to be taught by teachers according to guidelines arising out of adult analysis of the teacher of literacy rather than an analysis of how children conceive of reading and writing. Although there have been people who have disagreed with such beliefs those disagreements have usually been based on intuitive or moral reasons, or on limited individual experience.

Over the last ten years there has been a considerable increase in the amount of research investigating the pre-school child's knowledge of literacy. Contrary to conventional wisdom that children are unknowledgeable about literacy phenomena, it is clear that many, if not most, children have developed many skills and understandings about literacy. It is clear that the knowledge is not gained from artifically taught experiences, but from observation of, and interaction with, print and the people using it. This knowledge reflects the way adults use print purposefully in their lives. Children expect print to make sense in terms of their experience of the world.

By and large teachers do not take into account the fact that children have this experience. Far from building upon it, many teaching practices seriously distort children's existing and realistic conception of literacy. The kind of literacy curriculum most commonly found in schools ignores children's interests, knowledge and experience. It disconfirms their already established and reasonable expectations of what literacy is for and inhibits the development of accurate literacy concepts.

Utilising a wide ranging and deep knowledge of the relevant literature to underpin his arguments, Nigel Hall goes on to suggest that today's children are growing up in a world where print is more visible and making greater demands than ever before. The division between children's experiences of growing up in a print-rich environment and narrow, stilted, routine print-experiences of school life are increasing. If teachers really want children to be sensitive writers and readers, then they must adopt strategies which recognise and build on the existing sensitivities and avoid strategies which extinguish them.

These criticisms are also couched in positive terms in that the author cites a number of examples of teaching practices which <u>do</u> trade off and exploit children's literacy knowledge and skills which have been already developed outside the formal teaching situation. Such examples emphasise still more the imperative need for the literacy curriculum to be made relevant because children expect it to be. Schools cannot afford to turn children away from reading or writing. Unfortunately, that is exactly what happens to too many children by the time they leave primary school.

Chapter Six

PROBLEMS OF CHANGE, TEACHING AND CONTROL IN MIXED
ABILITY CURRICULA: A CASE STUDY OF INTEGRATED
STUDIES

John Evans and Brian Davies

INTRODUCTION

In this chapter we will report upon the endeavours
of one school, Sageton, a large, urban 11-18,
co-educational comprehensive school (cf Evans, 1982a;
Davies and Evans, 1984), to effect mixed ability
teaching[1] . The focus of our analyses will be
upon the actions of 'social science' teachers at
Sageton, and their attempts to effect curriculum
change by <u>individuating</u> (see below) their curriculum,
in respect of mixed ability grouping in the context
of lower school 'Integrated' and 'Related' studies
schemes of work. Our contention is that much of the
current practice of mixed ability teaching, as represented in the Sageton data, is often very far
removed from the kind of rhetoric and images of
practice outlined or intended in the egalitarian
prescriptions of educationalists and politicians.
Given the present conditions of their work, especially in respect of the pressures of time, for evaluation, order and control, teachers lack opportunity,
vocabulary and practice to effect the kind of mixed
ability <u>teaching</u> which would begin to look like an
effective and appropriate means of delivery for mass
<u>education</u>.
        Elsewhere we have discussed (cf Davies,1977,
Davies and Evans,1984) the variety of methods and
motivations which underlie a school's decision to
'go mixed ability'. At Sageton, as elsewhere,
mixed ability innovation was the product of rapid
school demographic transformation and senior management decision by fiat. Against this background,
it is not difficult to understand some of the
limitations which subsequently emerged in the subject
by subject classroom practice of many teachers and
their concomitant disaffection with mixed ability

grouping as an organisational practice.   As others
have pointed out (Bailey and Bridges, 1983, p.5)
'the teachers most deeply disillusioned with mixed
ability grouping are those in schools which have
taken the first steps (the decision to go mixed
ability grouping) without giving proper consideration to the second' (the meaning of mixed ability
teaching). But the despondency amongst teachers
vis-à-vis mixed ability teaching/grouping and $_2$
its subsequent demise in many secondary schools[2]
cannot we suggest, be fully appreciated or understood
only with reference to initial motivations. Close
examination of the process and practice of content
and method innovation subsequent to the mere change
in grouping is both necessary and vital if we are
to understand the limits, possibilities and precise
nature of the educational change being affected and
its implications for pupils and teachers.

THE INTEGRATED SCHEME IN SOCIAL SCIENCE AT SAGETON:
BACKGROUND

Academic organisation at Sageton took the form of
a faculty system. Each incorporated several
departments whose autonomy flourished more strongly in
the middle and upper school but which were curtailed
in the pursuit of thematic 'relevance' in the lower.
Such was the case in respect of the Social Science
faculty in 1977 where the time allocated for
'Integrated Studies' in each of years one and two,
and 'Related Studies' in year three, was 210 minutes
per week. In year one, upon which this discussion
will very largely concentrate, the timetable was
blocked to allow 6 x 35 minutes teaching units,
organised by the faculty into a block of four plus
two. The general pattern of teaching involved
a lead lesson, always a film with a half year group
of about 95 pupils. After the film the film half year
group divided into their respective tutor groups
(e.g. class 1P, 1Q, 1R, 1S). Each class then
received 35 minutes each of General (where it was
intended to follow up the film) and then History
and Geography lessons. Later in the week each class
received 35 minutes each of Multi-cultural Studies
and Religious Education.
     In year two a similar approach was adopted
except that the timetable was not 'blocked' and
the specialist subject requirements of the four
departments (History, Geography, RE, and Multi-
cultural Studies) were accommodated by a complex
alternation within a unit on a weekly basis. In

year three the autonomy of subject departments was
partially re-affirmed. Pupils received 70 minutes
each of History, Geography and either Religious
Education or Multi-cultural Studies, the latter
sharing time on a half-termly basis. Subject conten
were 'related', that is to say, drawn up in the knowledge of what was being taught in other departments
but the sequencing of units characteristic of teachine
in years one and two was absent. In years one
to three the curriculum and mode of presentation
was individuated, that is to say all pupils simultaneously had access to the same subject content
within common time limits defined by the syllabus
organisation and timetabling. Both factors (content
and time) were made available through work sheets,
from which pupils were expected to work alone and
largely independently of the teacher. The content
of the courses in years 1-3 came towards the 'newish
end of the spectrum and reflected aims more generally[3]
expressed in the wider subject sub-culture of
social science teaching[4].

> 'I think it's important to give pupils a
> world picture. We are so interdependent
> now. There's no point in concentrating
> only on Britain'. (Head of Faculty).

To this end, pupils in these years were introduced
to a series of weekly contents, contributed by
each of the departments and organised around a particular geographical location (a continent) and withir
this a theme or country[5]. For example, in year one,
term one, the first four weeks were located on the
continent of Africa (sic). The general theme was
'Tribes'. Each week was accounted for by an input
(in the form of a worksheet) from each of the departments. Hence the week 1: Lead lesson was a film on
the 'Evolution of Life, Man'. Geography contributed,
'Map of Africa. Location of the main Tribes'. The
History input was 'The Archeologist, what he does'.
Religious Education focussed on 'Animism', and Multi-
cultural Studies attended to 'Nomadic and Settled
Culture'. Subsequent weeks had similar pre-defined
contents for transmission, each embodied in the form
of a worksheet. Knowledge within a subject was intended to develop cumulatively in breadth and depth
but was not linearly sequenced from the point of
view of any one of them.
       From this brief outline we can see that the
scheme imposed a variety of constraints on the
teachers' pedagogic role. Not only was the

curriculum pre-defined for them, but also the pedagogical mode of its transmission. The syllabus
thus established for both teachers and pupils
precisely defined parameters of time and content
in which to work. Indeed, a situation had arisen
in which broad aims had been translated into a
series of precisely defined contents for transmission.
These in turn had been transposed to worksheets and
had, in effect, become the syllabus, a situation
not unlike that described by Hamilton (1976, p.200).
For the teachers concerned, theirs was a task of
ensuring worksheet completion on a 35 minute unit
weekly basis in order to ensure simultaneous progress
with adjacent subject contents.

Problems of pacing within the individuated
scheme, given that pupils related differently to
content in the time made available, were 'resolved'
at the preparation stage, either by pitching work
on the worksheets at various levels, or by providing
additional tasks for the 'able' pupil to complete.
Inherent to either resolution was a pacing of work
which necessarily ensured that not all pupils could
enjoy the satisfaction of worksheet completion.
This problem was most acutely felt by teachers of
first year pupils compelled to work within what
was felt to be the insufficient 35 minutes per
'subject' imposed by the scheme. Achieving task
completion amid increasing problems of control
pushed teachers to articulate this problem of time
as one of time-tabling rather than that of curriculum
organisation. Consequently its resolution was seen
to lie in a future re-negotiation of the time made
available (to allow 40-45 minutes) rather than in
a re-consideration of the structure inherent in the
syllabus itself. From the pupils' point of view,
learning constituted getting to the facts presented
by the worksheet in the limited time made available.
Each worksheet was self contained, though occasionally drawing on textbook material. Learning normally
merely implied finding the answers by simply reading
the material presented by the worksheet. Answers
were already there, to be uncovered by reading the
relevant text[6]. Sometimes an answer meant simply
filling in the right word. Teachers were occasionally heard to indulge in the ancient rite of encouraging pupils to 'answer the question in sentences' but an overview of exercise books revealed
a notable absence of this in practice. Within the
frame of limited time and pressure for task completion, the temptation to provide such material
as to ensure 'progress' reduced knowledge in

109

workbooks to a meaningless array of incomplete information.
     This situation had arisen because of the limits
of teachers' capacities to mount qualitatively effec
ive short run responses to changed circumstances
not of their making. Understanding 'integrated'
social science at Sageton requires us to delve deepl
into the paths which change followed, and the conditions which framed observed practices within the
school context.

PATHS TO CHANGE: FORM BEFORE CONTENT

The integrated scheme described above was not the
first attempt at 'integration' within the Faculty
of Social Science. In 1975, one year following the
inception of mixed ability grouping, a move had been
made towards integration in the first year. A Head
of Integrated Studies was appointed. However, the
motivation for change did not emanate from senior
staff within the faculty but from a group of junior
staff. In consequence the newly appointed Head
of Integrated Studies was in an unenviable position
of attempting to impose a 'new' integrated curriculum favoured by junior staff on senior colleagues who
had deeply established and antagonistic identities[7].
In a very short time the innovation had been thwarted
     A year later with the departure of this first
Head of Integrated Studies and the appointment of
a second, a further attempt to effect change was
made. A 'totally different set up' organised on a
'topic basis' was introduced, but this too had
broken down by the end of the first term.
     It was into this context of abandoned innovatio
that the current Head of Faculty had entered in 1977
He had arrived supportive of mixed ability and
inclined towards curriculum change

> I wanted to link together subjects.
> Where I taught before there was no
> link up. I don't think there's anything
> to be learnt in isolation. There's
> no point in doing different things, and
> at different times......'

He found however, that

> 'things were in a mess. The integrated
> studies syllabus wasn't workable. It
> was just a piece of paper. It was too
> difficult for the staff and kids. We

110

'**introduced** a pilot scheme.....changed
about Easter, a kind of introduction
to what we were going to do. We had
meetings, Heads of Departments got
together to discuss things. Geography
was non-existent, no syllabus, no books
and x still here as a deposed Head.
The thing was, to have framework.....'

The integrated scheme (outlined in the previous
section) was thus adopted and it had several
advantages. It enabled this teacher to realise
his intention of forging links between subjects.
It also effected greater control over other
teachers. The initial concern was essentially
pragmatic, to impose a coherent framework on the
anarchy of method and content which had emerged.
Hence the emphasis upon structure rather than
content:

'This year we're going to get the
structure right.   Then we can sit
down and think about the content'.

Moreover, the curriculum changes introduced avoided
problems associated with integration which had
thwarted previous attempts at innovation, that is
to say, they allowed teachers 'to teach their own
subject', (Head of Faculty), thereby retaining
specific subject identities and power domains.
But the demands of the timetable, together with
an insufficient supply of teachers to ensure that
each class could receive a subject specialist
on every occasion, still meant that teachers had
to teach a subject other than their own with
implications, as we see below, for their instruction
and control. However, the 'new' course structure
had neatly accommodated the authority of the Heads
of Departments and the integrity and identity of
their subject disciplines along with faculty management concerns for keeping control over more uniform
teaching method and content.   Thus there was little
initial opposition to the new course structure.
     The innovation resolved these problems, but
others, were immediately created. The teachers
themselves focussed on the workload, the time and
exhaustion involved in establishing the course,
particularly the preparation of materials and
worksheets, in respect of which they had insufficient
time to 'do a proper job'.

111

'The aim was to have the whole first
term's work produced by the Summer
term. We had one and a half hour
meetings a week to decide what
we were doing, then we just had to
produce the stuff'. (Head of Integrated
Studies)

The large area (years 1-3) over which change was
effected and the highly structured nature of the
course (compelling the production of worksheets
on a weekly basis) furthermore exacerbated teacher
problems of this nature. Even after the production
a sufficient quantity of materials to permit the
introduction of the course, teachers remained
concerned with what seemed to them an endless
production of the next worksheet. As this teacher
of Integrated Studies remarked, 'the problems have
remained the same.....getting the worksheets in,
preparation, getting them prepared in time'.
        The significant point here is the way in which
such problems, experienced at this second level of
management and preparation, subsequently operated
as frames (limits) upon <u>ability</u> in the teaching
process. At Sageton as elsewhere, the immediate
tendency in the production of worksheets, was to
reproduce within them a conception of ability and
teaching characteristic of traditional whole class
method.   Teachers had neither the time nor the
knowledge to plan and prepare otherwise. A common
solution to the 'problem of mixed ability grouping'
was the production of class material pitched at the
ability median of the class with extra materials
(usually open-ended tasks) being provided for the
able to keep them occupied until new contents are
introduced. The problem of 'pitch' also figured
in the readability of the worksheets. Analyses
suggested their suitability for pupils with a reading
age of twelve and above. This difficulty in their
accessibility was often exacerbated by the extremely
poor quality of their legibility and presentation,
largely contingent upon either limited teacher time
or technical inexpertise. As one teacher remarked,
'In the future we hope that all our worksheets will
be typed' (Head of History). The scheme thus implied
not only a level of pacing but also a level of
ability/literacy required to work within the limited
time available. With some 34 per cent of Sageton pupil
having reading ages on entry of below 9, many were
certain to find the material on the worksheets
difficult, perhaps incomprehensible and extremely

112

frustrating within the pacing of the courses. Beneath the surface appearance of innovation very little change had thus taken place either in teacher conceptions of pupil ability or teacher ability to produce materials varied enough to match its presenting character.

Factors other than time and expertise further limited teachers' opportunities to invoke more substantial educational change. A further problem in the teachers' perspective centred upon the levels of resource available to them and the cost (financial and time) of producing sufficient material for each of the pupils to have 'his own worksheet'. This meant that lesson time often had to be given to the task of 'copying out the questions' (from the work sheet) for homework as there were insufficient worksheets for every child to take one home. This practice not only further encroached upon scarce time, but also removed from pupils their source of support and knowledge, necessary for later 'getting the right answer'. This was a further source of antagonism and frustration particularly for those pupils whose pace through the worksheet was such to provide limited access to its contents.

> 'When we have to do homework right....
> we don't actually know something,
> right.....well we just have to leave
> it out we don't get a full mark for
> it....so we just leave it out....'
> (Pupil 17, 1P).

Time, at the second level of interaction and decision making, operated as a frame on teacher action, and subsequently on pupil ability, in another way. As one teacher remarked:

> 'What we do isn't integrated studies
> it's related studies. There's serious
> deficiencies of time, there's not
> enough time to talk about the scheme
> or the topics, or for departments to
> discuss how to draw out the inter-
> relationships'.

and another

> 'Theoretically Geography, History
> lessons are based on the film, but
> there's no meeting for second year
> integrated studies teachers, so it

> can't be. It's a mess. So departments
> know who's producing the materials in
> their subject but don't know who's
> producing the other worksheets. You
> just go to the box and get it out.....'

The problems here are indeed complex, and in part
arise from a disjuncture between 'integration'
as an idea, forced into co-existence with a perfectly ordinary subject-based staff and curriculum organ
isation. Without an appropriate organisational
structure supportive of new curricular intentions,
opportunities for teachers to plan, develop and
institutionalise integration in worksheet materials,
were severely restricted.[9] Following the establish
ment of themes and structure at a senior management
level, departments worked independently of each othe
producing relevant 'related' contents. In effect,
the organisation tended to ensure the systematic
development of contents <u>within</u> departments, with
only the most tenuous of links <u>between</u> subject
contents. Consequently, the degree to which pupils
perceived 'relatedness' in the course contents reste
upon teacher endeavours to draw out their connection
during lessons. As we see in the statements above,
the teachers' opportunity to provide this sort of
instruction were very limited at the second level.
Without organisational means of departmental co-
operation, yet with each teacher often expected to
teach a subject other than his own, a tendency
toward pedagogical instrumentality was inevitable.
That is to say, teachers had little choice but
to 'go to the box and get a worksheet', thereafter
transmitting information which was pre-coded for
them and about which little, if anything, was
known.[10] The separate subject bits of the curriculum remained as effectively separated for them as
for pupils in what continued to be a 'collection
code'. (Bernstein, 1977). For the pupils concerned
Integrated Studies certainly represented a limit
on ability not only in the form of time, level
and quantity of transmission, but also in respect
of its subject contents which together tended to
lack sense, coherence and meaning. They provided
a rich source of frustration and boredom.

> 'We work from worksheets all the time,
> every time, just like maths... work cards.

> All that rubbish....I don't like it....
> it's all muddled up.....I don't under-
> stand it.......' (Pupil 17, 1p).

and

> 'It's rubbish guy.....jumble....I'd
> prefer to do history, geography and
> ......like that......' (Pupil 6, 1p).

These problems of integration experienced by
teachers, could be seen to go far deeper than that
of the course <u>organisation</u>. There was as yet no
clear principle of integration to guide content
selection such as would force departments together.
Against the historical background of Social Science
teaching at Sageton however, this sort of luxury
was not immediately possible, but was considered
as a future focus for change. 'We have worked out
the structure, now we can sit down and start to
work on content, slant our work towards each others
work' (Head of Faculty).

But as one teacher noted:

> 'At present the themes seem to be
> chosen by Departmental Heads and
> Faculty Heads. It appears quite
> arbitrary. It might be better if
> we could reflect on the themes, why
> it's chosen. At present it doesn't
> appear that this is so'.

Integrated in name but not in organisational
structure, decision making remained firmly in the
hands of senior teachers. Teachers could feel
remote from areas of decision making concerned with
crucial matters of curriculum goals and course
organisation. They were expected to engage in
intra-departmental co-operation concerning the
production of worksheets/contents only after newly
articulated overall goals had been set. Ironically,
'integration' of this form had made the arena of
decision making more remote from teachers, the gap
between senior staff and the majority greater than
had previously been the case.
It is, perhaps, not surprising in respect of
what has been said, that teachers of Integrated
Studies were found to be experiencing problems of
pupil control. Enough has been said to suggest
that the limits of time, presentation and content

would ensure that learning for some pupils would be extremely problematic, a frustrating and unrewarding experience, as these statements (from pupils of class 1P and 2P) indicate:

> 'They're so short, you don't get time to finish the lesson. We're in the middle of a lesson and we're interested and we are told to go to see the film... then it finishes.....'

> 'They take the whole lesson reading out the worksheet and then the rest of the lesson is too short. If you had two lessons....normal like maths and English that would be all right'.

Of course not all pupils would experience this time factor as a frame, as limit, given their appropriate ability and willingness to work. Some, however, unable to enter successfully into the teaching process increasingly expressed their disaffection in active and difficult forms of behaviour.
Organised into four 35 minute units, Integrated Studies also created added occasion for pupil movement between lessons and increased interactional opportunities for indulgence in interest (i.e. non-work) activity during the merging of two classes for the lead (film) lesson. With the significance of films not always apparent to children and their growing awareness that the content of subsequent lessons could be coped with largely independent of attention during film lessons, the teachers' problems of achieving pupil order, became steadily worse, as even the first term in a year progressed.
Problems of teaching, learning and control were thus established for teachers and pupils outside the classroom at the department and faculty level of decision making. Mixed ability teaching as embodied in the syllabus realised a change in course structure rather than content. This change was necessary in order to effect control and some continuity over teachers and method. Given this structure teachers at Sageton as elsewhere had neither the time nor the expertise to fully consider or appreciate what mixed ability teaching might mean in terms of an educational practice capable of reaching and teaching the full range of pupil abilities and predispositions with which they are confronted. Nor could they be expected to, given the manner in which mixed ability grouping had been effected at Sageton. As Davies,

(1977) has argued, teachers tend to know far more clearly what they are changing from than what they are changing to. In such conditions, problems of control, which mixed ability at Sageton was meant to assuage continued to emerge across a far greater range of classrooms than had previously been the case under setting.

TEACHING AND LEARNING IN THE INDIVIDUATED CURRICULUM

In these conditions, teachers devised a number of strategies to reduce their problems of instruction, management and control. In classrooms, control is exerted through interaction in specific ways with individual pupils or with the class as a whole. In this respect with the problems of lead lessons and changeover (outlined above), teachers vigorously 'policed'll corridor behaviour, while in some second year classrooms opportunities for movement were removed altogether, the teachers preferring to 'team teach' rather than provide occasion for disorder. The emergence of this latter form of 'new' teaching was thus motivated by concerns for control rather than by anything like a more progressive pedagogical philosophy or any purely 'educational' rationale. Organisational decisions taken at levels outside the classroom thus became foci for the hidden curriculum.

In total some 28 first and second year and 16 third year lessons were observed. On no occasion was a teacher of Integrated Studies observed to deviate from the course structure, or fail to use its 'recommended' mode of transmission. Table 1 provides some examples of the temporary structure, over 3 x 35 and 2 x 70 minute periods respectively, in five first and second year classrooms. Table 2 refers to contrasts in the talk of first and second year teachers of Integrated Studies within the phases of time outlined, excluding settling and closure phases. Each count (in Table 2) refers to one complete interaction and not a specific speech utterance. Each interaction potentially carried a number of messages, disciplinary, diagnostic etc.

TABLE 1   Contrasts in the Temporal Structures of
           Five First and Second Year Teachers'
           Lessons (of 35 and 70 minutes respective-
           ly).

TEACHER, CLASS AND LESSON OBSERVED *	PHASES IN MINUTES			
	SETTLING	INTRO-DUCTORY	PUPIL WORK	CLOSURE
Ms Bodie 1S (Geography)	4	5	20	3
Mr Richards 1S (History)	3	10	18	4
Ms Lewis 1P (General)	5	6	20	4
Ms Newman 2P (Multi-cult-Studies)	8	14	40	7
Mrs Day 2P (Religious Inst)	5	30	30	5

* Case study groups followed at length across the
  curriculum in each year are always suffixed P.

TABLE 2   Contrasts in the talk of First and Second
           Year Teachers of Integrated Studies During
           the Introductory, in brackets ( ), and
           Pupil Work Phases of the lessons Described
           in Table 1.

TEACHER, CLASS AND LESSON OBSERVED	PUBLIC (talk to the whole class)		IMMEDIATE (talk to individual pupils)	
Ms Bodie 1S (Geography)	(1)	4	(4)	10
Mr Richards 1S (History)	(2)	5	(5)	35
Ms Lewis 1P (General)	(3)	4	(8)	12
Ms Newman 2P (Multi-Cultural Studies)	(2)	12	(–)	14
Mrs Day 2P (Religious Inst.)	(4)	3	(20)	16

Table 1 shows quite clearly that pupil work dominates
most classes and in the examples given in Table 2 that
most teacher talk is immediate, that is to say, it is
oriented to individual pupils while they work rather
than to the whole class (either as a class or to
individuals in the hearing of the whole class).
This is markedly different to that which we would
expect in whole class teaching, though it reveals more
teacher centralisation of talk than is the case in
our report drawn from the same classes working in
individualised[12] instructional modes like SMP Maths
(Corbishley et al 1981). In second (as in third)
years with larger (70 minute) work periods, there
tends to be more class instruction, more teacher
talk. Mrs Day with 2P is a clear case of this,
dividing time evenly between introductory whole
class instruction and pupil work (30 minutes each ,
Table 1) and also effecting more individual interactions 'in the hearing of the whole class' during
the introductory phase than were effected 'privately'
in pupil work time, whether control or instruction

oriented.

While these examples are offered as cases of arithmetically-frozen ethnographic variety, they need setting against a very similar general pattern of lessons, which can be characterised as follows:

Firstly, there was a settling phase character-ised by the establishment of an explicit positional frame of teacher control when worksheets were ad-ministered. Against this background there was an introduction of the worksheets to pupils. Their contents were read either by the teacher or selected pupils or the task was shared and elaborate or clarified (usually to resolve problems of poor presentation) either through the media or teacher talk or question-answer sequences. The latter displayed features typical of whole class method[13]. Questions were characteristically 'closed'. Answers could be guessed, or required little more than an ability to recall information previously acquired. Hence, a display of ability was contingent upon a willingness to conform to rules of attention/con-centration. What counts as knowledge was confined to the parameters of factual content defined by the syllabus. Questions were steered by the teacher's concerns for what is functionally necessary to reduce immediate and pressing problems of instructio (pacing, coverage) and control. These features are further elaborated and exemplified below. This phase was followed by a period of individuated pupil work. In this respect (see Tables 1 and 2) Integ-rated Studies classrooms were far less 'busy' places for teachers than those of individualised instructio e.g. in SMP workcard Maths. Generally, there were fewer instructions at an immediate face-to-face level and fewer public regulatory messages. Teacher tended to take one of two roles during this phase. Firstly, and more prevalent, they took a supervisory role (Ms Bodie with 1S, Ms Lewis with 1P and Ms Newm. with 2P), characterised by an explicit positional frame of control, the teacher taking up a front of class position, interacting with few individuals unless called upon to do so either in response to a pupil's appeal or instances of difficult behaviour Secondly, as exemplified by Mr Richards with 1S, to a lesser extent, by Mrs Day with 2P, they displayed an interactional role, where the pupil work phase was characterised by a period of intense 'busyness' as the teacher did the rounds. These differences, cannot simply be reduced to differences of teacher 'philosophy' in terms such as the tradi-tional v. the progressive. Indeed, as we see, the greater contrast in philosophy was between Ms Bodie and Ms Lewis whose actions in the classroom firmly achieved a marked similarity. Regularities in the actions of all these teachers are, we would suggest, functional expressions of a situation in which they find themselves. On the one hand, teachers control the teaching process at classroom level, resolving or attempting to resolve problems of discipline, pacing, content. On the other, teachers are themselves controlled or constrained by related factors, by the interplay of pupil identity, content, time and mode of transmission. Discipline and instruction are concretely structured in interaction in specific ways, with specific groups of pupils.

Some examples from the practice of these teachers will highlight the relationship between the limiting features of curricula outlined above, and the teaching process, along with the opportunities for the imposition of idiosyncratic teacher styles.

Ms Bodie and Mr Richards, both senior teachers committed to further development of the Integrated Studies scheme and (with some reservations) mixed ability teaching, were responsible for teaching the pupils of 1S. They 'team taught' only in 'Films', with Ms Bodie subsequently teaching the General lessons, Mr Richards the History lesson, and finally Ms Bodie returning to teach the Geography lesson. Eleven of the pupils of 1S have reading ages below 10, 3 of whom are Asian pupils with very little ability to speak English. Both teachers were concerned about problems of instruction and pupil control. In lead lessons (Films) a number of strategies to resolve their problems were in evidence. The settling phase characteristically began with the teachers dividing their labour so that Ms Bodie took up a supervisory role while Mr Richards ensured the readiness of the projector etc. This was followed by a brief 2-5 minute introduction of the film contents, and involved little more than a brief reminder of what had previously been seen and what the day's viewing was to consist of. For example:

'Today we're going to look at Egypt, at the Egyptians, at the Oasis, all the people who live around them. How they live.....methods of cultivation......'.

This opening was followed by an attempt to further delimit the focus of the film, (which tended to be of a general type covering an area of content far wider then prescribed by the syllabus) to

contents known to be connected to subsequent worksheet contents, e.g.

> 'I want you to note in particular.....
> irrigation - why it is used?......'

and followed by appeals for order in the form of
procedural statements:

> 'If you don't follow now you won't know
> what to do in the classroom.....'

What we would suggest is in evidence here is an
expression of structural constraints (the syllabus
and a large crowd of pupils) in the form and conten
of teacher talk. The teacher defines what it is
to be learnt, what is valid knowledge and extracts
from the range of opportunities the film presents
knowledge of subsequent significance for worksheet
completion. Without a knowledge of subsequent
contents other than those for which they are directly
responsible, teachers tended to further restrict
their talk to specific subject areas. During a
film, for example, (in a lesson of Miss Bodie and
Mr Richards):

Teacher:	'What's in the bags?'
	'If it's a hot climate what are you going to lose a lot of?'
Pupil:	'Hair!'
Teacher:	'Through the skin?..... Salt.....So what's going to be important?'
Pupil:	'Salt'
Teacher:	'Salt....Yes....So what do you think is in the bags?'
Pupil:	'Salt'
Teacher:	'Yes.....good.....salt'.

Pupil contributions are typically short, and
guided toward slots in a developing exposition[14]. In
an obvious sense, these features of talk in lead
lessons, resolved both instructional and regulatory
concerns. Classroom order related to the teachers'
success at establishing the significance of lead

122

lessons for subsequent lessons. Some pupils however recognised the limited importance of these lessons and increasingly displayed difficult behaviour. Indulgence of such behaviour (facilitated by the darkness demanded by films) appeared as a supportive controlling strategy.

General lessons, which preceded or followed lead lessons emerged as occasions of strategic importance for teachers such as Ms Bodie and Mr Richards. This time was used either to re-introduce worksheets previously unfinished or introduce a worksheet for completion in subsequent lessons. Rarely was time used as intended to 'follow up' i.e. discuss the contents of films observed. This strategy reduced a teacher's problems of pacing and task completion but, interposed between lead and follow-up History and Geography lessons, further undermined the significance and coherence of the work in the pupils' perspectives:

> 'But after we do the film right....not
> always....right....we don't do the same
> thing about the film because they don't
> talk about the film'

Factors other than time, however, underlie a teacher's decision to behave in the manner described. Ms Bodie notes:

> 'Ideally this period would be used for
> discussion of the film, but you can't
> do that with pupils like P and D present.
> They are so unpredictable.....you can't
> risk it.......'

Control was sought in those activities which offered greatest structure and opportunities for surveillance of pupil behaviour by the involvement of all pupils with the worksheet, rather than in the single person verbal exchange of class 'discussion'. Occasionally however, the latter was attempted by Ms Bodie:

> Teacher: In the film we saw some mounds –
>   what were others called..... Brian?
>
> Pupil: Pardon Miss?
>
> Teacher: ((repeats))
>
> Pupil: Dunes

Teacher:	˙Yes...why can't people go around in bare feet?
Pupil:	It's too hot....they get burnt feet
Teacher:	Yes ((elaborates))

This somewhat mechanical questioning of pupils continued for 25 minutes. There was no exchange of information or expression of opinion on the part of pupils and consequently no indication or impression of the problems they may have experienced with the film were revealed. The orientation in language was towards assessment, rather than reply.[15] Insight or 'knowledge' was not required of pupils beyond levels of attention to and recall of previously accummulated contents. Moreover, a cursory glance at the distribution of communication in this lesson revealed that the 'able' child (as defined by teache ratings) accounted for the greater part of individua communication with the teacher. Eight pupils accounted for 26 of the 39 'bids' of responses to teacher questions, while another 6 took the remainin 13. The latter pupils, amongst the least able and most problematic to the teacher, were controlled by their teacher-initiated involvement in instructional talk. The mixed ability grouping had brought about few changes in the structure or content of classroom discourse. It was controlled by the teacher and steered by the syllabus content, its pacing defined with reference to the able child. Individual differences amongst pupils initially brought to the context were thus likely to be confirmed.[16]

Subsequent History and Geography lessons taught by Mr Richards and Ms Bodie had many of the features already described. In their History and Geography lessons described in Tables 1 and 2 the introductory phase was characteristically short, though significantly Mr Richards spent almost twice as much time as Ms Bodie on this phase. Little attempt was made to show connection between specific worksheet contents and the structure of the course as a whole. Talk was restricted to clarifying immediate contents, to ensuring sufficient understanding for 'progress', i.e. worksheet completion in the phase of pupil work. Pupil 'progress' was further facilitated by the act of 'doing first questions', or even all of them on the worksheet, the teacher either providing answers or stressing how or where they may be found in the text. In this way a teacher's immediate management problems were reduced. Such a rigid definition of what constituted 'finding out' was represented in all classrooms observed.

In the phase of pupil individuated work, however, differences between Ms Bodie and Mr Richards had emerged. Ms Bodie's approach was characterised by a supervisory role. Once the introductory phase had been completed, it was largely assumed that the worksheet was sufficient for pupils to progress. Like others, she 'did first questions' thereby reducing immediate demands upon herself to resolve individual learning problems. Further problems had little scope in which to flourish as a particular worksheet 'lasted' for only a single period. Next week brought a repetition of the same limited sequence in which this teacher's concern focussed predominantly upon maintaining classroom order. In the lesson described (Table 2) she interacted with 9 of the 20 pupils present for instructional purposes on 10 occasions during the pupil work phase. Her interactions were characteristically and pervasively drawn towards the actions of pupils considered most difficult to control, a role quite consonant with her more general approach, features of which were rigorous and public enforcement of a positional frame of control. Throughout the lesson, pupils were left in no doubt as to the asymmetry of relationships which obtain between them and teachers and her commitment to imposing the course upon them in its existing form, of 'making it work'. In the settling phase, for example, talk was characterised by harsh imperatives and positional appeals:

> 'What a stupid lot you are.....sit
> down....am I going to wait for you
> to settle down? .....Hurry up.....
> OK....turn to your worksheet.....'

Thereafter 'silence' was called for while selected pupils read the text. In contrast to this somewhat autocratic approach, the actions of Mr Richards appeared as altogether more 'liberal'. Control (to use Bernstein's notion) is less visible, boundaries between lesson phases are more obscure and hold over pacing, within the limited time permitted, more relaxed. For example, in an introductory phase, the teacher announced:

> 'OK....those who wish to read....listen
> now....if you're happy carry on....if
> not listen.....'

Against a background of positional control explicitl
announced in initial encounters (e.g. in asking
pupils to stand on teacher entry), this teacher,
in the above manner, was able to reduce his problems
of instruction, pacing and control. By allowing the
'able' to proceed alone, the less able received
the necessary clarification of content, though
their problem of worksheet completion was still
not resolved. Furthermore, in the interest of
maintaining order and securing completion, this
teacher placed a premium on interaction at an
immediate face-to-face level, as we see in Table 2.
Such actions can be seen as reflections of the
teacher's educational beliefs and perception which
give him a characteristic interpretation of the
constraints of classroom practice. Both teachers
expressed a commitment to mixed ability grouping,
Ms Bodie because of

> 'the detrimental effects of selection on
> those who don't get into the top streams'

Mr Richards because in

> 'mixed ability, you've got to teach as
> a class of individuals. They've got
> to be known and related to individually....
> but the possibilities of this? The amount
> of energy needed is terrific. How to
> recognise 2 or 3 pupils all likely to
> be a control problem. Fiona for example....
> you let them get on with it a little in
> respect of the group and you come back
> to them.....to get them going'

We might infer that Ms Bodie believes the 'work'
of mixed ability innovation to be accomplished
when streaming is abolished. Nothing else follows
in terms of a need to alter pedagogy. Mr Richard's
justification for mixed ability is in terms of the
utility of a more individual pedagogy and an attempt
is made to reform teaching action in consequence.
      Time remained for this teacher an acutely scarce
commodity. Given the pupil demands emergent in the
classroom context which he permitted (with a weaker
frame of control than is evident in the action of
Ms Bodie),his ideals could hope to be realised only
via the expenditure of considerable energy and an
amount of 'indulgence' of otherwise deviant behaviours. This teacher was 'oriented towards being a
class teacher' and to getting things moving via his

own initial talk in which a display of teacher
enthusiasm was perceived as crucial to pupil
motivation.   It was in the act of 'doing the
rounds' that he consequently attempted to achieve
a great deal of individual contact only to be inevitably constrained by the worksheet as a mode of
transmission in the limited time.   As Barnes (1977,
p 137) points out, worksheets 'interposed between
the teacher and the pupil will tend to minimise the
likelihood that the teacher's interests in the subject
matter will be communicated to his pupils'.   In doing
the rounds (and during introductory phases which,
as we see (Table 1) were longer than those of Ms
Bodie) a 'performance' was given in which the salient
qualities appear as dynamic enthusiasm, humour and
interest for the subject.
      The behaviour of both these teachers represent
strategic responses to experienced structural problems, mediated by individual perception.   Both
teachers were 'successful'in establishing order
and appearing to be productive within the
structure of the integrated course.   Ms Bodie contained learning problems within the frame of positional control which involved more public regulation
rather than immediate (instructional) intervention.
Mr Richards in contrast used a wider variety of
strategies.   He invoked a more 'informal' control
over pupils, relaxed control over pacing, displayed
interest and provided help at an immediate level.
Thus he was able to facilitate a degree of pupil
progress, though of a limited kind given the brevity
of such interactions.
      Ms Lewis with 1P, in contrast to each of those
teachers, equated mixed ability with 'a more flexible
structure'.   'If a child asks a question and it
doesn't know the answer, it doesn't seem relevant...
and it could contribute, it could be a learning
situation for all of them.   Then I think you should
accommodate it.'   At the same time she was aware of
constraints in the form of a wider framework of expectations which defined teaching and learning in a
way contrary to her own, which limited opportunities
to effect this sort of teaching.

> 'The only problem in mixed ability is
> very.....sort of.....tends to be a very
> informal way of teaching.   To teach
> informally you have to have an informal
> structure.   This school doesn't have
> that.   It's very formal.   If your
> children are noisy in a lesson or

127

if they seem to be enjoying themselves
then people who are passing your classroom might say that you had no discipline...'

In contrast, to both previous teachers mentioned,
Ms Lewis in initial encounters with the pupils of
1P, tried to use General lessons as intended in
the course.

(A)	Ms Lewis:	today....I don't want to do any writing...we are going to have a discussion. I want to know what you thought about the film....
(B)	Jerry:	((copies the teacher))....I want to know what you thought about the film?
(C)	Ms Lewis:	Colin! What do you think of the film?
(D)	Jerry:	It was about Egypt and the River Nile. How people get water from the river .
(E)	Ms Lewis:	.....right....yes.....what did the water do for them?
(F)	Jerry:	Grow crops....
(G)	Ms Lewis:	Good....is he right? .... We saw it was barren, in the desert, you just can't produce water. How did they get water.....?
(H)	Fiona:	I don't know .
(I)	Ms Lewis:	Look listen....listen to what others have to say....
(J)	John:	It was rubbish.....
(K)	Ms Lewis:	Why is it rubbish...come on....that's a silly thing to say....give a reason....
(L)	John:	I can't understand a word they're saying

(M)	Ms Lewis:	Move......Jerry....
(N)	David:	It's a stone age country
(O)	Ms Lewis:	Explain....
(P)	David:	They didn't wear modern clothes, they were primitive people.... they lived in mud huts...

The teacher has to intervene in the growing non-work activity of pupils (.....'I'll wait a minute to see how quiet you can be. Ryan can't be quiet....OK. Odette give out the folders.....I wasn't going to do any writing but you can't be quiet....')
Ms Lewis attempted to use the time available for lead lessons in a way quite contrary to that of Ms Bodie. Her action reflected her belief that it was important to define the situations in such a way that more 'open' forms of communication were possible. Indeed difficulties were revealed in John's answer(L) and prejudicial attitudes in David's reply (N), which would not have surfaced in more typically 'closed' communications. It became apparent, however, that as the frame of teacher control over knowledge was relaxed, disciplinary problems increased. Engaging in this form of communication, Ms Lewis assumed that pupils are able and willing to interpret this form of questioning as meaningful and therefore act in the desired way. While some pupils were able to respond in the desired way, others found such talk tangential to the task of getting work done.

Jerry remarks:

'We didn't do any work just talk.....
and then she's always moaning at you......'

Ironically such teacher action <u>generated</u> difficult behaviour. For it was to those very pupils who expected a strong positional frame of control (in this case, the least able pupils and those pupils defined by the teacher as able but difficult and underachieving), that such 'open' questions were addressed, in an endeavour to <u>maintain</u> order. Consequently, in subsequent lessons observed, the teacher was less inclined towards this form of discussion, there was more work from worksheets and discussion of a type earlier outlined and she adopted a supervisory role, characteristic of that described

in relation to Ms Bodie.   In the General lesson
outlined in Tables 1 and 2 for example, Ms Day
interacted with only 10 of the 19 pupils present for
instructional purposes on 12 occasions during the
phase of pupil work.   Her actions were steered
by the disciplinary problems presented by the less-
able and able-but-difficult pupils of the class.
These two categories account for over half of the
immediate contacts.

Ms Lewis' endeavours to step outside the structure
of the scheme with Class 1P thus were limited not onl
by content   and time but also by the pupils themselves.   As Barnes (1977, p.127) has noted, they
have learnt during the years that most teachers only
wish to hear the expected reply, but they do not
want discussions 'that include divergent viewpoints
and which raise different questions from theirs'.
Given that the pupils in 1P routinely experience
a supervisory style of teaching in Integrated Studies
and with other subject teachers, it would be most
surprising if this teacher were able to 'bring off'
successfully the kind of approach she ideally
desired.

If nothing else, innovation at Sageton left the
normal forms of school action untouched.   Once the
course content was produced in the worksheet,
there was nothing else for teachers to do other than
secure its transmission, revise or 'improve' its
messages.   As one senior teacher noted:

> 'Well it seems to have become a bit
> too easy....you get teachers just
> going to the box before the lesson
> and taking a worksheet....That's it....'

Once established the courses took on an existence
largely independent of teachers, who were required
only to oversee their servicing and management.
These feelings could be particularly acute for
teachers such as Ms Newman who played no part in
course formulation and the production of worksheets.
Because most of her teaching was done in other
sectors of the school, she had little interest in
its practical or pedagogical outcomes.   In these
circumstances, the teacher ritually went through
the motions of implementing the course as she
received it.   As Tables 1 and 2 suggest, Ms Newman's
lesson pattern was straightforward.   During introduction of the worksheet, in order to keep control,
the teacher took full responsibility for its
'reading', followed by a lengthy period of pupil

work, in which a generally supervisory role was
assured. With little investment in such actions,
the outcome was as unsatisfying for Ms Newman as
it was for the pupils concerned.

DISCUSSION

For teachers such as Ms Newman with 2P and Ms Lewis
with 1P, the curriculum package along with the
expectations of pupils and significant others within
the organisation, could arguably be seen to have
had a de-skilling effect upon them. Certainly,
neither was able to teach in a way they would like.
However, given the general conditions of schooling,
the inflexibility of the timetable and pupil
expectations, limited resource, pressures for
control and effective evaluation, along with the
limited expertise of teachers regarding how to teach
heterogenous abilities, then to talk of such curricula as
requiring only new skills of management or control
in the way, for example, Apple (1980) does, is both
unhelpful and certainly misleading. The adoption of
such new curricular forms can and should, we contend
(cf Evans 1982a) constitute a re-skilling of teachers,
not only in terms of classroom practice but also in the
organisation of curriculum (time, content, pedagogy)
at departmental and faculty levels. Both preparation
and use of workcards and worksheets with a mixed
ability range requires no less but rather different
skills from teachers, to an extent as yet barely[17]
realised either by themselves, inspectorate
or analysts of their classroom tasks. Effective
direction of the workcard mode minimally requires
from teachers an ability and willingness to admit
pupils to greater degrees of insight and self-control
over their means of knowledge acquisition, which
would presuppose quite transformed insights into the
nature of modes of transmission on the part of
teachers themselves, as well as resources to effect
appropriate change.
   Some negative indication of the kind of skills
required of teachers at classroom level may well be
found in the actions of teachers described above.
But the analyses can hardly stop there bearing in
mind that the actions observed to a large extent
represent available coping strategies, the means
by which these teachers attempted to resolve and
reduce problems associated with a course which
they had rapidly constructed, or others had constructed
for them, to meet specific organisational ends. None
of these teachers would consider themselves to have

achieved effective mixed ability teaching. It would
be an odd analysis, indeed, that judged them to
be 'deskilled' on such a timescale. What we can
say is that mixed ability teaching in this context
had certainly provided few opportunities for success
for the less able pupils.   An ability/willingness
was required for all pupils to cope with content
more or less independently within quite limited
periods of time.   Many pupils without appropriate
pre-dispositions and procedural abilities found the
worksheet mode of transmission difficult and unrewarding.   As their difficulties with managing the
means of learning (including making its regular
interruptions appropriately available for teachers'
remediation, that is to say, getting help when stuck)
was expressed in difficult behaviour, they were
imputed deviant as well as 'less able' identities.
    It is perhaps not surprising then that the
successful teacher in the perspectives of pupils,
in this context, is a teacher neither 'radically'
inspired (who attempts to step outside the structure
of the course and generate 'new'knowledge) nor
overly 'autocratic' (able to impose the course
in its existing form, upon pupils), but one whose
'liberal' endeavours permit pupils a degree of 'working within' the limits and constraints on ability
imposed by the course organisation and structure.
Mr Richards of 1S and Mrs Day of 2P provided interest
ing work, help and understanding, broke the routine
of working with their enthusiasm or humour and therel
facilitated some degree of progress.   Of course, not
all pupils experienced the conditions of learning as
restrictive.   Those who had the predispositions to
work within the limits imposed tended to pos-
itively appraise teachers.   For the able pupils of
class 1P, for example, Ms Lewis is neither considered
too soft, nor unable to provide the required attentic
(even though during classroom time they receive less
attention than the less able and active).

> 'She's the best.....kind...she's nice and
> makes us think we'll learn good things...
> doesn't just keep on saying shut up and
> be quiet all the time.....' (Naren).

For those unable to meet the requirements of
learning, however, and dissatisfied with the
teacher's approach, the unchanging conditions of
practice give rise only to a mutual and negative
identification.   Taking this view, we would suggest
that pupil deviance and alienation often stems not

from a confrontation of reified knowledge, but from their problems of <u>access</u> to it. Hence, the 'good' teacher performs in such a way as to provide 'help' and 'understanding' of contents and her control is 'fair' and 'strict'. His or her humour also needs to be sufficient to break much of the routine and boredom associated with learning. These teacher behaviours, however, are not unprogrammable attributes of individuals. They are structured responses to concrete situations. They can be planned for and produced.

However, it would be difficult to argue then that within comprehensive schooling, mixed ability grouping at Sageton brought about any great net advancement towards greater educational opportunities for all pupils. Many of the features described in this individuated scheme are also represented in the group-based and individualised curricula in other subjects and have been evidenced in studies of other schools (cf Ball, 1982, Goodson, 1975, Corbishley et al, 1981). Such new departures represent very little change in the deep structure of educational codes, in how teacher's conceive of and use time, ability, content when altering modes of transmission. Consequently, such new modes continue to impose constraints upon teacher's <u>action</u> in the sense defined by Lundgren (1977), Barnes (1977) and Edwards (1980), in respect of the form and content of classroom discourse and in the teacher's use of time. Teacher talk is steered by the syllabus, pupils' behaviour, and organisational expectations, rather than by an interpretation of pupil ability or educational need or interest. Individual differences between pupils are those reinforced in the interaction pattern which may functionally resolve a teacher's instructional control problems but leave largely untouched a pupil's learning needs. Innovation is effected without change, pupils continue to fail and are alienated from teachers, schooling and the learning process, while we absolve our lack of control over this failure by reading it as either a direct result of pupil psychological/social deficit; or the hit or miss of teacher personalities, or, even more absurdly, of investing differentiated school knowledge with some pupil-alienating property.

NOTES

1.   This paper refers to materials which is
part of a broader study of mixed ability grouping
and curricula, funded by the SSRC in two stages as
A Preliminary Study of Unstreaming in London
Secondary Schools and Teacher Strategies and
Pupil Identities in Mixed Ability Curricula: a case
study.   We would like to thank the SSRC for supporting these projects.
2.   The incidence of mixed ability grouping has
almost certainly been on the retreat since the late
70's.   Its 'shape' from first to third years in
secondary schooling is reported in Reid, et al (1981)
3.   A term used by Ball (1981, p.182) to refer
broadly to 'the professional self image' of the
members (teachers) as subject specialists and particularly views of teaching current within the subject
4.   See, for example, in Williams, M.(ed) (1976)
5.   See Elliott, G.(1974) for a critique of this
form of 'integration' and the role of Geography
within it.
6.   See also Edwards and Furlong (1978) who
portray this form of learning as a feature of first
year Humanities teaching at the Abraham Moss Centre.
7.   As Musgrove (1976, p.134) points out 'subjects are not only intellectual systems they are
social systems: they confer not only a source of
identity in their members they confer authority and
they confer power'.
8.   Hargreaves, A (1978, p.92) discusses the
use of homework as a coping strategy.   Without
sufficient resource and opportunity to set homework, teachers at Sageton were limited in their
capacity to use this means of coping.
9.   Hamilton (1976) discusses the problems of
managing 'mixed' integrated and collection curricula
in Integrated Science teaching.
10.   In this way worksheets provided a necessary
substitute for any 'deeper' integration, forming the
point of contact between departments.
11.   The elements of which are described by
Hargreaves, A. (1979, p.146).
12.   In individualised instruction where all
pupils are working on worksheets or cards on potentially different topics at their own pace, class
instruction is rarely possible.   Much of the teacher's
time is spent interacting with individual pupil's
privately at the pupil's or teacher's desk.
13.   See Edwards, A.D. and Furlong, V.J. (1978)
for a discussion of what research has shown to be the

134

characteristics of classroom talk.
    14.   See Edwards 1979 .
    15. A characteristic feature of transmission teaching, Barnes, D. (1977, p.111).
    16. Merely transposing the frame of teacher control to worksheets in an individuated curriculum, does little then, to attentuate outcomes which, as Lundgren (1977) describes, are characteristic features of class teaching.
    17. Bailey and Bridges (1983, p.46) make the point that Her Majesty's Inspectorate seem to assume (Department of Education and Science, 1978) that teachers could competently teach not merely all levels of ability, but all levels of ability together.

REFERENCES

Apple, M., (1980) 'Curricular form and the logic of technical control: building the possessive individual' in Barton, L, Meighan, R. and Walker, S. (eds) Schooling Ideology and Curriculum Change, Falmer Press.

Bailey, C., and Bridges, D. (1983) Mixed Ability Grouping: A Philosophical Perspective, London, George Allen and Unwin.

Ball, S. (1982), Beechside Comprehensive, Cambridge University Press.

Barnes, D. (1977), From Communication to Curriculum, Harmondsworth Penguin Books.

Bernstein, B. (1977), Class, Codes and Control Vol. 3 Towards a Theory of Educational Transmission, 2nd Selection, London Routledge and Kegan Paul.

Birt, D.(1976), 'All Ability History' in Teaching History, Vol IV, No.16, 1976, 309-325.

Buswell, C. (1980) 'Pedagogic Change and Social Change' in British Journal of Sociology of Education 1. (3) 293-307

Corbishley, P. Evans, J. Kenrick, C. and Davies, B. (1981) 'Teacher Strategies and Pupil Identities in Mixed Ability Curricula: A Note on Concepts and Some Examples for Maths' in Barton, L. and Walker, S. (eds), Schools, Teachers and Teaching, Falmer Press, 177-179.

Davies, (1977), 'Meanings and Motives in going Mixed Ability' in Davies, B. and Cave, R.G. (eds), Mixed Ability Teaching in the Secondary School, London, Ward Lock.

Davies, B., and Evans, J. (1984) Mixed Ability and
    the Comprehensive School in Balls (Ed) (1984),
    'Comprehensive Schooling : a reader, Lewes,
    The Falmer Press.

Edwards, A. (1980), 'Patterns of Power and Authority
    in Classroom Talk' in Woods, P (Ed), Teacher
    Strategies, London, Croom Helm.

Edwards, A., and Furlong, V., (1978), The Language
    of Teaching, London, Heinemann.

Elliot, G. (1974), 'Integrated Studies – Some Problem
    and Possibilities for the Geographer' in
    Williams M(Ed) (1976), 160-166.

Evans, J., (1982a), Teacher Strategies and Pupil
    Identities in Mixed Ability Curriculum : A Case
    Study, Unpublished PhD Thesis, Univ. of London.

Evans, J, (1982b), Teaching Control and Pupil Iden-
    tity in Mixed Ability Curricula: A case study
    of Science teaching paper presented to the St.
    Hilda's Oxford Conference on Histories and
    Ethnographies of School Subjects September
    1982.

Goodson, I., (1975), 'The Teachers' Curriculum and
    the new reformation', Journal of Curriculum
    Studies, Vol 7., No.2, November.

Hamilton, D. (1976),'The Advent of Curriculum Integ-
    ration : Paradigms last or Paradigms regained?'
    in Stubbs, M., and Delamont,S. (Eds), (1976),
    Explorations in Classroom Observation, London,
    Wiley and Sons.

Hargreaves, A., (1978),'The Significance of Classroom
    Coping Strategies' in Barton, L, and Meghan, R.
    (Eds), (1979), Sociological Interpretations of
    Schooling and Classrooms: A Reappraisal,
    Driffield, Nafferton 73-109.

Hargreaves, A., (1979),'Strategies, Decision and
    Control: Interaction in a Middle School
    Classroom' in Eggleston, J (Ed), (1979),
    Teacher Decision-making in the Classroom,
    London, Routledge and Kegan Paul, 134-190.

1. Reading and writing are primarily visual-perceptual processes involving printed unit/sound relationships.

2. Children cannot be ready to learn to read and write until they are five or six years old.

3. Children have to be taught to be literate.

4. The teaching of literacy must be systematic and sequential in operation.

5. Teaching the 'basic' skills of literacy is a neutral, value free activity.

These assumptions, albeit sometimes unspoken, could not resolve the problem of how to teach reading, not did they make teaching reading easier. However, they did provide security; they marked the boundaries of the teacher's task and controlled some of the associated phenomena.

The view that children were not ready to learn to read and write until they were five or six years old, and that they had to be taught to read and write, clearly elevates the status of the teacher. Helping children to become literate was a task for the specialist - not the parent. That reading and writing were conceived of as visual-perceptual processes involving printed unit/sound relationships enabled the creation of elaborate sets of rules governing the order in which these relationships had to be taught. Once the rules were clear the teaching of these rules became an activity akin to a science, understood by most teachers to be a context free, neutral activity. It also meant that as a complex set of rules was elaborated the specialist nature of literacy teaching was confirmed. The child was seen as an object having few skills which could be processed by the specialised knowledge and skills of the teacher into becoming literate. As many children were not too competent at coping with the myriad of skills, the belief in children's literacy incompetence was reinforced.

Thus whether the teaching was based on phonic, alphabetic, whole word, or sentence methods of reading instruction, certain elements remained unchanged. Control of the manner and rate of learning was firmly in the hands of the teacher. It was the teacher's task to move children from a state of being a non-reader and non-writer, to being

someone who possessed mastery over the skills
involved in being literate. The children's
role was to follow that route from start to, with
luck, finish.

Inevitably there have always been people who
have conceived of the task, and the role, in
different ways, and there have always been children
who arrived in school with literacy skills. The
stance of the teaching profession has been to
dismiss such children as wholly exceptional, so
much so that their existence has always merited the
special attention of educationalists (Torrey 1969).
Unless such abilities were very clearly visible,
however, schools, ensconced in their traditions,
frequently failed to discover the skills possessed
by some children:

> That Laura could already read when she went
> to school was never discovered! 'Do you know
> your ABC?' the mistress asked her on the
> first morning, 'Come, let me hear you say
> it: A- B- C-'
>
> 'A- B- C-' Laura began: but when she got
> to F she stumbled, for she had never memorised
> the letters in order. So she was placed in the
> class known as 'the babies' and joined in
> chanting the alphabet from A to Z.
>
> (Thompson, (1973, p.183)

A more up-to-date example would be those children
whose readiness to read is evaluated by their
performance on visual discrimination exercises in
pre-reading material. As Clarke in a study of
young fluent readers clearly demonstrated (1976,
p.32), 'It is possible for even young children to
become very fluent readers in spite of an average
or below average ability to reproduce or even to
remember in their correct orientation, isolated
designs sufficiently clearly to identify them from
a range of alternatives'. Or finally, the six year
old who said 'I know this word is 'dog', and I
could read it even if the picture wasn't there,
but I don't understand what I'm supposed to do
with this 'dee', and 'oh'· and 'gee' the teacher
keeps talking about'.

A CHALLENGE TO THE ASSUMPTIONS

This 'rule-bound' and 'teacher-controlled' stance

Downing's statements are about what children cannot do. However as Goodman (Gollasch,1982, p.25) suggested, 'if anyone sees a half-empty glass adjust the focus so that it appears half-full'. He went on to say 'we're going to be content with what is present and not be distracted by what is not'. He elaborates on the image in a later paper (Goodman 1976, p.23) when he claims 'I think it is symbolic because it says we have been too pre-occupied for too long with what children cannot do, what they are not ready to do, what they don't care to do. We have lost the significance of what they have going for them that we can build on.

In 1976 when Goodman wrote those words they were mostly a political statement about a belief in children's competence. Since that time, stimulated by the works of the Goodmans, researchers have begun to pay considerable attention to children's competence. Paradoxically, as Downing's work has developed he has, perhaps unwittingly, been demonstrating more and more the competence of children to perform his tasks.

The emphasis in these more recent investigations is much more on devising ways of assessing competence and much more on observing children as they deal with things in their normal worlds. To some extent competence in reading has been a subject of study for many years. This 'competence' research has been about those children who arrived at school demonstrating ability to read. Torry (1979) reviews studies into 'early reading' and suggest that such behaviour was, anyway, more common than generally believed. However, of the eleven studies cited by Torrey all, save three, gathered their data about the pre-school behaviour of the 'early readers' after the children had started school; the remaining three studies gathered their pre-school data after the children had been identified as early readers. In a major British study (Clarke,1976) information about pre-school literacy behaviour was also gathered retrospectively. While such studies are informative they were not designed to support the implication of Smith and Goodman's work that, given appropriate conditions, almost all children will naturally develop strategies towards, and understanding of, print.

THE CONTEXT OF EARLY LITERACY COMPETENCE

That pre-school children do possess competence in literacy skills has now been demonstrated by researchers operating in different countries and with

different social groups. Such a statement is
not meant to imply a state of definitive knowledge.
The nature of the studies and the range of questions
to which they address themselves inevitably mean that
so far only a start has been made. However, the logi
of the demonstration is quite clear. The claim that
most children have little or no knowledge about
literacy is easily refuted if most of the numerous
children studied do demonstrate a range of competencies with literacy.

There are a growing range of studies of individual children (Lass,1982 and 1983, Bissex,1980,
Calkins, 1983,Butler,1979, Payton,1984, Crago and
Crago,1983, Torrey,1969), which show that these
children not only possess an exciting range of
literacy competencies, but that they are also active
participants in constructing their knowledge. As
Goodman (1984, p.108) put it, 'children seem to work
through some of the same problems that the adult
inventors of written language historically have had
to solve, such as the way to display letters and how
to organise the writing into units'. For the childre
in the above studies, literacy was not a decontextual
ised activity but an intrinsic part of activities
that were meaningful in their own right. Such studies
are extremely provocative in suggesting developmental
processes. However, they inevitably engender certain
types of criticism: with the exception of one study
(Torrey,1969) all the researchers studied their own
children and those children were obviously middle
class, educated families. It would, however, be a
mistake to assume that the performance of these
children were simply a case of being exceptional
children. Those children may well be bright but it
is probably more important to consider the environment rather than heredity. All these homes nurtured
what Goodman (1980) calls the 'roots of literacy'.
That is, they gave opportunities for the children
to participate in meaningful literacy events, they
provided environments where there was considerable
talk about literacy, and responded sympathetically
to the children's developing intuitions about the
forms and functions of written language. The
purposeful and print-rich environment of those
children is in marked contrast to the print environment provided by many schools.

There are. two studies which go well beyond the
study of the individual pre-school child. The
books by Ferriero and Teberosky (1980) and Heath
(1983) are seminal works in their field. They
adopted rather different strategies, that of

Ferriero and Teberosky being a Piagetian experimental approach and that of Heath being an ethnomethodological 'community watching' approach. Yet the picture that emerges from both studies is of children who are active participants in constructing an extensive pre-school knowledge of literacy.

Ferriero and Teberosky set their study closely within a Piagetian framework. Indeed theirs is about the only study which starts with a solid theoretical position. They set out to identify those constructs about literacy which appear consistently yet could not have be taught or borrowed from adults. Their subjects were 4-6 year old, middle and lower class Argentinian pre-schoolers. They examined the children's understanding of the formal features of the graphic system (letters, numbers and punctuation) the differentiation between text and pictures, the children's interpretation of reading acts and the evolution of writing. They concluded that even at the youngest age group all the children understood that writing is not just lines or marks but a 'substitute object representing something external to the graphics themselves'. They identified what they call 'two outstanding characteristics' of the way children develop literacy. The first is that children, within their own notion of the rules of literacy, are remarkably consistent in the way they follow rules. The second is the internal logic of the progression. Pictures are distinguished from non-pictures before there is any attempt to distinguish between aspects of non-iconic graphics. Once that distinction is clear then children turn their attention to the elements of print, learning to distinguish between letters, and letters and non letter literacy marks. Ferreiro and Teberosky's analysis makes it clear that 'progress in literacy does not come about through advances in deciphering, copying, or teaching'.

The rather strict Piagetian framework limits the focus of this research and it says nothing about the social conditions under which literacy skills develop. Heath (1983) spent ten years observing, in the main, two small communities in the South of the United States. Neither community was of the educated middle class that features so highly in most American educational research. Yet within these communities Heath found that there was extensive participation in literacy by pre-school children, although the styles of involvement were quite different (a point also noted in the work of Schiefflin and Cochran-Smith, 1984). In both

communities, although there was no direct teaching
of pre-school literacy, the children grew up as participants in the literacy process of the community;
they were expected to do so.

Heath says of the pre-school children in Trackton (a working class black community), 'the children
read to learn before they go to school to learn to
read' (p.191). She notes, (p.192), Trackton children
are sent to the store almost as soon as they can walk
and since they are told to 'watch out for Mr Dogan's
prices', they must learn to read price changes from
week to week and remember them for comparisons with
prices in the supermarket'. The children are not
specifically tutored in these skills by any form of
school-like instruction. 'Young children watch
others read and write for a variety of purposes, and
they have numerous opportunities for practice under
the indirect supervision of older children, so that
they come to print independently and to be able to
model appropriate behaviours for younger children
coming up behind them' (p.192).

In the studies mentioned here, and in the many
studies referred to in Goelman, Oberg and Smith
(1984) it is usually the dynamic, purposeful nature
of the print environment and the interaction between
participants which is memorable. As Heath points out
about the Trackton print experience, 'Certain types
of talk describe, repeat, reinforce, frame, expand
and even contradict written materials, and children
in Trackton learn not only how to read print, but
also when and how to surround the print in their
lives with appropriate talk'. (p.196).

The dynamic and purposeful nature of family
print experience is beautifully represented by the
Bulletin board kept by one family observed by
Leichter (1984,p.44).

> Their bulletin board, largely maintained
> by the mother used print to organise the
> family's life in terms of its basic concerns.
> An ERA (Equal Rights Amendment) button, news-
> paper clippings, and cartoons were reflections
> and reminders of the mother's newly acquired
> political and feminist beliefs. A green
> plastic shamrock and some St. Patrick day
> cards were a display and reminder of the
> family's ethnic identity. Cards for other
> holidays served to organise and reinforce
> other ceremonial events within the calendar
> year. An envelope for coupons and an unem-
> ployment book were reminders of the economic

reality of the family's life. An appointment
card for visits to the pediatrician and dry-
cleaning slips helped organise memory. The
eldest daughter's successful school report
and her scores in a bowling tournament in which
she did particularly well attested to special
achievements of family members. Notes of
apology or notes saying 'I love you' reinforced relationships or attempted to ease
inter-personal problems. Wedding pictures,
pictures of family friends, and a card that
the daughter had drawn for her mother served
to commemorate special occasions. Fliers,
posters, pamphlets, leaflets and notes telling
of school board elections, plays, athletic
events, and children's entertainment helped
the family keep track of community events.

Children in this family could hardly doubt the
interest, the importance and the multitude of
functions of literacy.

So far most of the research reported has been
from outside Britain. This almost inevitably reflects a failure on the part of British researchers
rather than any comparative inadequacies on the part
of British children. These few people who have
begun to examine the area (Payton, 1984, Fox, 1983,
and Dombey, 1983) have found similar areas of pre-
school literacy knowledge.

Fox (1983) examined the extent to which young
children's story telling abilities was influenced
by the books they had read to them. She came to the
conclusion that children 'can and do learn complex
rules of narrative production before they can read
and write, rules which we are sometimes more
accustomed to find underlying the texts of mature
adult writers'.(p.24) She gives an example in which
one child uses appropriately, in the first seven
utterances of a story, seven different literary
modes. The skill of such children and their experiences with a multitude of pre-school texts which
contain numerous literary conventions certainly
call into question the monotonous diet of many reading scheme books on which infant children are fed
(Grunden, 1980) and on which many junior children
continue to feed (Southgate-Booth, Arnold and
Johnson, 1981). As Fox states 'The majority of
such books come nowhere near using the many narrative
conventions children can learn just by listening to
good stories read aloud and they are even further
away from the literary competencies the children are
acquiring' (p.24).

Payton (1984) in her study of the developing literary awareness and competence of 'Cecilia' demonstrates the active role of Cecilia in exploring literacy and linguistic aspects of her environment. Of particular importance in this account is the demonstration of the richness of the print environment in which Cecilia was growing up. Cecilia's first literacy comment was to point to a label and remark correctly, 'that says Co-op'. No one had asked her and no one had told her. It appears to be a genuine dedication. As Payton (p.28) points out, 'what had been discussed in many typical everyday conversations were the day's shopping requirements, where they were to be purchased, how the journey should be made and so forth that is the contextual information'. Within such contextual and, more importantly, purposeful situations the three 'roots of literacy' identified by Y Goodman (1984) can grow.

THE LITERACY CONTEXT OF SCHOOL

It would seem that on the whole children do not arrive at school ignorant about literacy. They are not empty vessels waiting to be filled by teachers. Many will have developed an extensive range of understandings about the nature and purpose of print. Children will have developed this knowledge not from teaching but from observation and thought about contextualised literacy events. Indeed the literacy is an almost incidental by-produc of more purposeful activities. As Schieflen and Cochran-Smith (1984, p.7) put it, 'Literacy events consistently were embedded within the social interactions of adults and children. For participants, the literacy events themselves were not noteworthy'. Within these 'social interactions' children will have demonstrated that they had internalised many of the rules and rituals associated with literacy skills Of course the knowledge about literacy possessed by children will vary. However the essential point is that there will almost invariably be some level of skill and knowledge. It is the level of knowledge which can, and should, act as the starting point for school instruction.

But what actually happens when children go to school? Are children able to develop their internalisation of the ways of using reading and writing by having such skills modelled for them or explained by adults in schools? Are they going to be exposed to environments in which they can develop

their knowledge of the contexts in which print could
be used, of the purposes which print could fulfil
and of the ways in which print could be interpreted
in relation to its context? Are the children going
to be able to sort out their own rules for interpreting
and using print-effectively by organising it for their
own social purposes? To these points derived from
statements by Sheifflen and Cochran-Smith (1984)
others can be added: Will the school literacy
environment enable children to understand that
'literacy events function not as isolated bits of
human activity but as connected units embedded in
a functional system of activity generally involving
prior simultaneously occurring and subsequent units
of action'?   (Anderson and Stokes,1984, p.28). Are
children going to be exposed in infant schools to many
of the fifty types of print encountered in homes by
Leichter (1984), or participate in events as dynamic
as that example of the bulletin board cited earlier?
Will children be able to develop awareness of their
literacy decisions, to change their perceived errors
and to capably self select a set of things upon which
they know they need to work? (Harste, Burke and
Woodward 1981).

   In many British schools the answer to all these
questions would seem to be a resounding 'no'. The two
most recent observational surveys give a disturbing
picture of institutions which, far from opening up
options in literacy, operate effectively to close
them down. The survey Reading competence at 6 to 10
(Hodgson and Pryke, 1983) was carried out in twenty
Shropshire Schools and includes such statements as:

> Clearly the most favoured method shown
> by this sample of infant teachers was
> direct intervention when a child made
> a decoding error (p.9)

> There is little evidence of the use of
> context or any engagement with the
> child in the discussion of the meaning
> of the text (p.10).

> We were tempted to wonder whether children
> who were showing competence merely demonstrate
> fluency despite rather than because of the
> presence of their teacher (p.14).

> There is very little evidence of any sort of
> contextual approach to the teaching of reading
> (p.15).

165

The whole activity seems to be conducted
in a perfunctory manner where the main
objective is to hear the next child
read (p.15)

There was no indication that any of the
teachers interviewed perceived reading as
a process (p.34)

Indeed the methods they adopt, because they
are essentially mechanistic, often militate
against the child actually enjoying reading
(p.35).

These statements indicate vividly the failure on the
part of these schools to provide mental space, social
interaction, or encouragement as far as reading is
concerned. At least twenty more similar quotations
(some worse) could have been cited and it is worth
pointing out that the authors of this study, as
employees of the LEA concerned, had no vested interest in damning their own schools. It is difficul
to conceive of anything as rich as Leichter's 'Bulletin board' occurring in any of these schools.

The second survey is that of Bennett, Desforges
and Cockburn (1984). They were investigating the
extent to which teachers in infant schools managed
to match the tasks they set to the needs of the
pupil. Bennett's sample was selected for him by Loca
Authority advisors who chose above average teachers.
His observations are concerned mostly with the teaching and development of writing. Amongst many re-
vealing quotations are:

There was no evidence of an integrated
language curriculum in operation in any
of the classrooms studied (p.99)

The predominant aim expressed in more
than 70% of tasks intended to promote
writing was to 'practise writing' and to
use some aspects of grammar, especially
capital letters and full stops as sentence
markers (p.101).

It was impossible to distinguish between
tasks aimed at developing imaginative writing
and tasks aimed at writing reports (p.103).

Finding the correct answers was exceedingly
straightforward and the vast majority of the

time on these tasks was spent recording
responses, a procedure which was little
more than further writing practice (p.119).

Frequently while the child read the
teacher attended to a queue of pupils
seeking assistance with their set work
(p.123).

Requests for spellings constitute the
predominant teacher/pupil exchanges in
language lessons (p.128).

It is impossible to read both of these surveys
without feeling the immense gap that exists
between the sparse, decontextualised environments
of those schools and the print-richness and
purposefulness of the pre-school experiences of
even the poorest children studied by people like
Torrey (1969), Clarke (1976), Leichter (1984)
and Jacob (1984). Schools in both Britain and
the United States seem very similar in the ways
they operate to deny the validity of children's
knowledge, skills and successful modes of learning.

CONCLUSION

It is no wonder that it is 'difficult to compare the
literacy skills involved in clipping, organising,
and placing coupons on a bulletin board, or in designing a poster to celebrate a family event, with those
involved in filling in blanks in a vocabulary note-
book' (Leichter 1984, p.44). It is no wonder that
Paul, a child who was at home, performing complex
phonic exchanges 'had a difficult time completing
workbook exercises the next year when he was in
first grade. The playfulness and sense of discovery
had gone and he was not interested in demonstrating
what he already knew' (Bissex, 1984, p.90). It is
no wonder that Jonathan who had been writing stories
which anyone could read came home after one week at
school refusing to write anything but his name.
'His response to the question 'why don't you write
a story', was 'I can't write 'til I'm in first grade'
And he didn't' (Goodman, Y 1980 p.3). It is
interesting to speculate on the extent to which these
three American examples have parallels in Britain.
   On the whole, schools provide neither a print-
rich environment, nor an authentic literacy environment. There has to be reasons why children use
written language and these reasons need to derive
from the purposeful nature of a whole range of

activities. Too many schools offer the children only one reason - the instructional one. You are here to learn to read and write and learn to read and write you will. Unfortunately, this instructional pose produces literacy lessons which are ends in themselves not means to a genuine social or personal end. The end points are success in handwriting, spelling, grammar, punctuation, filling in blanks, writing a page in thirty minutes, copying successfull from the blackboard, moving on to yet another book in a reading scheme. The end point is seldom genuine communication. Writing neatly becomes more important than making sense or being interesting.

Schools do not have to operate in ways which ignore the literacy strengths of young children. There are many schools which put great efforts into building an environment where the acquisition of further literacy skills takes place in a purposeful way. What is it that these classrooms do which so many classrooms, including it seems the ones observed in the two surveys noted earlier, fail to do?

These classrooms set out to create conditions which help children perceive the nature and purpose of literacy. They set out to avoid conditions which hinder access to such understandings. In particular teachers in such classrooms:

> help children to understand that print is about meaning and communicating meaning

> help children appreciate that literacy is a distinctly human activity. It enables people to communicate

> help children see that people engage in literacy acts because such acts are con- sidered important and useful by these people (including teachers')

> help children recognise that literacy is a means to many kinds of ends; that it serves many purposes and fulfils a wide range of real functions

> help children learn that literacy acts are pleasurable because they enable the satisfaction of a whole variety of personal and functional needs

> help children understand that their
> existing achievements in literacy
> are important and valued

> provide wherever possible activities
> involving the authentic use of literacy
> skills

The ways in which such classrooms might operate
have been documented by a range of people, Blass,
Jurenka and Zurgow (1981), Goodman, J, (1979),
Hall (1982), Anning (1984), Goodman and Goodman (1979)
and Wiseman (1984) amongst many others. All stress
supportive environments which are rich with purposeful
literacy incidents. These are not classrooms which
set up artificial barriers which hinder genuine
communication and understanding. Unfortunately,
it is often the case that teachers are either unaware
of, or ignore the fact that, children arrive with some
understanding that literacy is a useful and pleasurable
skill. As Y. Goodman (1984, p.109) states

> With this knowledge children enter school
> where, too often, they are placed in a
> rigid, instructional setting that ignores
> and is incompatible with what they already
> know. No published instructional program
> has ever provided the generalizations and concepts
> that people must develop to learn to read and
> write. A highly structured, instructional
> system that focusses on mastery of one rule
> or skill before another loses sight of the
> complexity of learning written language. It
> oversimplifies what children do learn and
> focuses some insecure children on insignificant
> and often erroneous principles about language.

Too often such systems of literacy instruction create
problems for teachers. When children become bored
reading basal series texts (Bettleheim,1980), write
only reluctantly (Graves,1983), or eventually
(as many children do) turn away from reading altogether (Whitehead,1971) teachers have to ask, 'how
can we motivate them?'. As Graves (1983) has
brilliantly shown, if you allow children to demonstrate
their competence, and support their efforts, motivation largely ceases to be a teaching problem.
Seventy per cent of Tasmanian teachers are now using
the 'process' techniques developed by Graves (Walsh
1984) and are finding that the change has a dramatic
influence on both students and themselves.

Children's self-initiated literacy competence is not
a myth. It is variable in both its level and the
rate at which it can develop. Schools must facilitate not stand in the way of children progressing
with a real sense of achievement through involvement in genuine literacy activities. It is worth
remembering, as Bissex (1984, p.100) comments,
'children are small; their minds are not'. Teachers
must build on and extend the literacy strengths and
knowledge that children already have, not ignore
and refute hard won abilities.

REFERENCES

Anderson, A.B., Teale, W.H. and Estrada, E. (1980)
   'Lower Income Children's Pre-School Literary
   Experiences', Quarterly Newsletter of the Lab-
   oratory of Human Cognition, 2, 59-65.
Anderson, A.B. and Stokes, S.J. (1984) 'Social and
   Institutional Influences on the Development
   and Practice of Literacy', in H. Goelman et al,
   op.cit.
Anning, A. (1984) 'Reading and Writing to some
   Purpose', Child Education, January.
Bennett, N., Dedforges, C. and Cockburn,   (1984)
   The Quality of Pupil Learning Experiences,
   Lawrence Erlbaum Associates, Hillsdale New
   Jersey.
Bettleheim, B. and Zelan, K. (1982) On Learning to
   Read, Thames and Hudson, London.
Bissex, G. (1984) 'The Child as a Teacher', in H.
   Goelman et al, op.cit.
Blass, R.J., Jurenka, N.A. and Zirzow, E.G. (1981)
   'Showing Children the Communicative Nature of
   Reading', The Reading Teacher, 926-931.
Brumbaugh, F. (1940) 'Reading Expectancy', Elementary
   English Review, 17, 153-55.
Butler, D. (1979) Cusha and her Books, Hodder and
   Stoughton, London.
Calkins, L.M. (1983) Lessons From a Child, Heinemann
   Educational Books, New Hampshire.
Clarke, M.M. (1976) Young Fluent Readers, Heinemann
   Educational Books, London.
Crago, M and Crago, H. (1983) Prelude to Literacy,
   Southern Illinois University Press, Carbondale
   Illinois.
Deny, T. and Weintraub, S. (1966) 'First Grader's
   responses to Three Questions about Reading',
   Elementary School Journal, 66, 441-448.

Dombey, H. (1983) 'Learning the Language of Books',
   in M. Meek (Ed.), Opening Moves, London Univers-
   ity, London, pp.26-43.
Downing, J. (1970a) 'Children's Concepts of Language
   in Learning to Read', Educational Research, 12,
   106-112.
Downing, J. (1970b) 'Relevance Versus Ritual in
   Reading', Reading, 4 (2), 4-12.
Downing, J. (1979) Reading and Reasoning, W. and R.
   Chambers, Edinburgh.
Downing, J., Ayres, D. and Schaeffer, B. (1983) The
   Linguistic Awareness in Reading Readiness Test,
   National Foundation for Educational Research,
   Slough.
Ferreiro, E. and Teberosky, A. (1983) Literacy Before
   Schooling, Heinemann Educational Books, London.
Fitzgerald, J.W. (1980) 'The child's perception of
   the Reading Process is Context Specific',
   unpublished Ph.D. Thesis, United States Inter-
   national University.
Fox, C. (1983) 'Talking Like a Book',in M. Meek (Ed),
   Opening Moves, London University, London,
   pp 12-25.
Goelman, H., Oberg, A. and Smith, F. (1984) Awakening
   to Literacy, Heinemann Educational Books, London.
Gollasch, F.V. (1982) Language and Literacy: the
   Selected Writings of Kenneth S. Goodman, Rout-
   ledge and Kegan Paul, London.
Goodman, K.S. (1976) 'Manifesto for a Reading Revolu-
   tion', in M. Douglass (Ed.), 40th Yearbook
   of the Claremont Reading Conference, Claremont
   Graduate School, Claremont, pp 16-28.
Goodman, K.S. and Goodman, Y. (1979) 'Learning to
   Read is Natural', in L. Resnick and P. Weaver
   (Eds.) Theory and Practice of Early Reading Vol.
   1, Lawrence Erlbaum Associates, Hillsdale New
   Jersey, pp. 137-154.
Goodman, K.S., Goodman, Y. and Burke, C. (1978)
   'Reading for Life: the Psycholinguistic Base',
   in E. Hunter-Grundin and H. Grundin (Eds.)
   Reading: Implementing the Bullock Report, Ward
   Lock Educational, London, pp.9-24.
Goodman, Y. (1980) 'The Roots of Literacy',
   in M.P. Douglass (Ed.), 44th Yearbook of Clare-
   mont Reading Conference, Claremont Graduate
   School, Claremont, pp.1-32.
Goodman, Y. (1984) 'The Development of Initial
   Literacy', in H. Goelman et al, op.cit.
Graves, D. (1983) Writing: Teachers and Children at
   Work, Heinemann Educational Books, London.

Grundin, H. (1980) 'Reading Schemes in Infant
    Schools', Reading 14 (1), 5-13.
Hall, J. (1982) 'Making Written Language Meaningful',
    Journal of Language Experience, 5, 14-18.
Halliday, M.K. (1969) 'Relevancy Models of Language',
    Educational Review, 22, 1-128.
Harste, J., Burke, C. and Woodward, V. (1982)
    'Children's Language and World: initial
    encounters with print', in J. Langer and M.T.
    Burke-Smith (Eds.), Reader Meets Author: Bridg-
    ing the Gap, International Reading Association,
    Newark Delaware.
Heath, S.B. (1983) Ways with Words: Language, Life
    and Work in Communities and Classrooms,
    Cambridge University Press, Cambridge.
Hodgson, J. and Pryke, D. (1983) Reading Competence
    at 6 and 10, Shropshire County Council.
Jackson, D. and Hannon, P. (1982) The Belfield
    Reading Project, Belfield Community Council.
Jacob, E. (1984) 'Learning Literacy through Play:
    Puerto Rican Kindergarten Children', in H.
    Goelman et al, op.cit.
Johns, J. (1970) 'Reading: a View from the Child',
    The Reading Teacher, 23 (7), 647-648.
Krippner, S. (1963) 'The Boy who Read at Eighteen
    Months', Exceptional Children, 30, 105-109.
Lass, B. (1982) 'Portrait of my Son as an Early
    Reader, 1', The Reading Teacher, 36(1), 20-26.
Lass, B. (1982) 'Portrait of my Son as an Early
    Reader, 2', The Reading Teacher, 36(7), 508-515.
Leichter, H.J. (1984) 'Families as environments for
    Literacy', in H. Goelman et al, op.cit.
Mason, G. (1965) 'Children Learn Words from
    Commercial TV', Elementary School Journal. 65,
    318-320.
Payton, S. (1984) Developing Awareness of Print:
    a Young Child's First Steps toward Literacy,
    Educational Review, University of Birmingham,
    Birmingham.
Reid, J. (1958) 'An investigation of Thirteen
    Beginners in Reading', Acta Psychologica, 14,
    295-313.
Reid, J. (1966) 'Learning to Think about Reading',
    Educational Research, 9, 56-62.
Schiefflin, B.B. and Cochran-Smith, M.(1984) in H.
    Goelman et al, op.cit.
Smith, F. (1971) Understanding Reading, Holt,
    Rinehart and Winston, New York.
Smith, F. (1979) 'The Language Arts and the Learner's
    mind', Language Arts, 56, 118-125.

Smith, F. (1981) 'The Myths of Writing', Language Arts, 58, 792-798.

Smith, F. (1982) Writing and the Writer, Heinemann Educational Books, London.

Southgate, V., Arnold, H. and Johnson, S. (1981) Extending Beginning Reading, Heinemann Educational Books, London.

Thompson, F. (1973) Lark Rise, Penguin Books, Harmondsworth, Middlesex.

Thorndike, E.L. (1917) 'Reading as Reasoning', The Journal of Educational Psychology, 8, 323-332.

Torrey, J. (1969) 'Learning to Read Without a Teacher', Elementary English, 46, 550-556.

Torrey, J. (1979) 'Reading that comes Naturally: the Early Reader', in T.G. Waller and G.E. Mackinnon (Eds.) Reading Research: Advances in Theory and Practice, Academic Press, New York.

Tovey, D (1976) 'Children's perceptions of Reading', The Reading Teacher, 29, 536-540.

Walsh, V. (1984) 'The Elephant and the Kangaroo: A Tasmanian Perspective on Early Reading', Paper presented at United Kingdom Reading Association Conference, Reading and the New Technologies.

Weinberger, T. (1983) Fox Hill Reading Workshop, Family Service Unit, London.

ISSUES IN EVALUATION AND ASSESSMENT

In this section, we have four contributions, each focussing on four different issues, all important in the life of schools.

In 'Consumerism for Curriculum Users', Digby Anderson suggests that teachers should regard themselves as consumers of curriculum goods. It is true that they do not buy them with their own money. It is also true they choose them for pupils. But it is teachers who choose from among the array of suggestions, packages and even orders that they receive from publishers, inspectors, superior teachers, advisors, politicians and parents. How do they and how should they choose?

He suggests that curriculum innovators some-times show irritation with the way teachers choose from within a supposedly integrated package. This and other evidence might suggest that teachers have a healthy scepticism when it comes to innovations, 'new' methods and revolutions in teaching. Like much in teaching, such scepticism is acquired by experience at work. Many new teachers have to un-learn their faith in various methods and curricula, a faith that was acquired during training. But it is possible to learn how to evaluate curricula pro-posals critically, sceptically but not dismissively before starting teaching. It is not necessary to await failure in the classroom before making a rea-sonable judgement on a particular package. What is needed is to ensure that part of a teacher's train-ing be learning to ask certain critical questions about the ever-proliferating array of suggestions, packages and advice which deluge teachers. His chapter deals in particular with one obstacle to curriculum evaluation - curriculum illusions.

Some curriculum proposals offer the teacher or appear to offer the teacher things he values.

They claim to be practical, not just theory. They
seem to be based on good research. He can empathise
with them. Their arguments seem sound. Yet all too
often these qualities are illusory for curriculum
designers have now become good at appearing to provide
what teachers want. The teacher or trainee teacher
choosing a curriculum needs then to know how to read
it so as to assess it realistically, in particular
how to counter or allow for its rhetoric of prac-
ticality, research and 'sound argument'. The chapter
looks at several curriculum proposals and shows many
of the ways in which the rhetoric works. The author's
aim is quite simple: to sensitise teachers to the
language, conventions and artful practices of the
curriculum market.

Hence the author explicitly utilises an econom-
ist's model for assessing curricular materials by
using the key question, 'what is the opportunity
cost of doing X?', i.e. what do I have to give up,
or forego, to do X, given that resources are limited,
and I cannot have everything. The next two contributors involve different kinds of models and arguments
in evaluating what goes on in the classroom, but both
are similarly acerbic and make constructive suggestions.

Harry Osser brings to bear psychological perspectives to analyse a crucial aspect of traditional
assessment procedures: finding out what pupils know.
In his view, these procedures are inadequate and pay
only lip service to the necessity of discovering what
the pupil knows as a basis not only for creating good
curricular materials, but also for any sustainable
notion of 'good' teaching.

He forcefully argues that standard psychometric
testing views the pupil as a passive absorber of
school-based knowledge and aims to measure the extent
to which it has been imbibed. Whereas clinical assessments are more sensitively attuned to the pupil's
actual stock of knowledge, wheresoever acquired,
and reveal much more about him and his problems as an
active learner. Although there is a place for
psychometric testing - when classification is all
important - clinical testing is more useful on a day
to day basis for assessing pupils' learning difficulties.

In a section which may concern many teachers, he
shreds away their taken-for-granted ability to
'know', on the basis of 'experience' and 'professional
expertise', what their pupils are doing. If these
skills are based mainly on the end products of pupils'
work, then it is more than likely that the processes

of learning are being overlooked.

Osser argues that a wider base of observation
is needed for assessing what pupils know than their
efforts to reproduce parts of the formal school
curriculum. To this 'academic' (or content) knowledge must be added consideration of the pupils'
'social-cognitive knowledge', i.e. their ability to
understand one another; and their metacognitive knowle
which is the pupils' ability to self monitor self cor

Using examples based on transcribed classroom
interactions between teacher and pupil, Osser shows
how a focus on metacognitive knowledge can serve to
bring out deficiencies in the teacher's understanding
of what the pupils know. For what the pupils are
making of what goes on, what meaning they are investing in classroom activities, is by and large a myster
to teachers. One way in is to try to discover those
areas in which any given pupil does observe close
self monitoring and those where casual monitoring is
adopted. It may be that these two different approaches are related to 'generative' (active, creative)
and 'formulaic' (rote) learning respectively.

John Robinson and John McIntosh, however, are
faced with the formal assessment of the products of
the formal school curriculum as the dominant influence
of their everyday professional life. As teachers of
'A' level Sociology in a Sixth Form College, they
have perforce to judge and be judged by the examination performances of their pupils. The fact that
these outcomes are important to them and to their
pupils provides the tacit underpinning to the framework of the argument they build.

Central to this argument is a note that will
resonate with many 'O' and 'A' level teachers - or
indeed most teachers with students sitting formal
examinations. This note is struck by the sheer
press of examinations to produce a type of outcome which may well not reflect the skills and knowledge best suited to the 18 year old school leaver.

Thus Robinson and McIntosh are concerned that
students acquire a range of practical skills and the
sorts of insights and understandings that can best
be derived from 'doing' rather than simply 'knowing'.
For them, Sociology is a practical subject necess-
itating the doing of empirical enquiries into the
workings of the social world. The unintended consequence of examinations can be to force pupils
into a seemingly 'scholarly' mould which boils down
to learning what one sociologist says about another,
rather than making direct enquiries into their own
social world. The sociological output of others

176

should be a means to this end, not an end in itself.

In their view, this problem is not confined to 'A' level sociology. Other subjects can, should and sometimes even want to develop in terms of encouraging pupils to exercise similar skills of practical enquiry.

That it is possible to do so - in sociology at least - is illustrated by the contrasting experiences of the 'hide bound' 'A' level students in contrast to some of their CEE peers. From observational reports and transcribed materials, the authors seek to show how CEE students produce more stimulating work owing partly to the greater freedom afforded by CEE Mode III type examinations and partly to the lower expectations by teachers of this type of student. Thus CEE pupils are not squashed because they cannot reproduce the correct vocabulary. Rather, attention is focussed on their grasp of what is being talked about. Whereas 'A' level students must produce the jargon if they are to be successful in the examination. As Robinson and McIntosh put it, '..."Knowing that" still appears to be more important that "knowing how"....'.

Like the last two authors, Tony Cassidy is also a practising teacher. But he is a practising teacher with a difference, for it has been his particular task to focus attention, heighten awareness and implement change in classroom methodology across the curriculum and across the school. To him has fallen the challenging task of solving the perennial problem of how to educate the educator! Somehow he had to find strategies for encouraging professional development, school-wide self-evaluation and a cooperative sharing of ideas and experience between the many and varying teachers that made up a large secondary school.

Needless to say, much of the resistance and problems came from the senior staff, the 'old hands' who know what is what and do not take kindly to the suggestions and implicit criticism of 'young upstarts'. To overcome such interactional problems requires no little ingenuity and improvisation, within the framework of support given by the backing of the headmaster, whose support is vital in the school context.

Tony Cassidy gives an enthralling and graphic depiction of what he had to do to overcome base problems. His account frankly details mistakes made and realistically assesses the impact and potential of the new approaches and thinking he pioneered.

On a personal note, both editors can vouch for

the accuracy of his account of events in the first
school he describes. We both attended the development sessions open to all staff. From our standpoint part of this session might be underplayed
a little. In it he had his team acting out the
transcripts of lessons, including all necessary
sound effects, and 'noises off' in front of the
whole staff. What emerged was plenty of good humour,
but also some considerable insight for many into
what lessons can look like 'from outside'. We
saw plenty of evidence for this sort of inference
in the ensuing small groups in which we also
participated.

Of course, the major thrust of the work in this
school was to bring to the fore what lessons might
mean and how they might be experienced by the
pupils, and transcriptions of actual lessons were
used to illustrate this point. In his subsequent
post in another school, Tony Cassidy is seeking to
diversify his methods in following this same end.
His title, 'Sweeping Porridge Uphill....' is ironic,
but not despairing. For in trying to make teachers'
normal, routine everyday practices 'anthropol-
ogically strange', he is taking positive action
to stimulate change through the insights that come
from self-realisation. For lasting effect, no
other route to change is viable or tenable.

not sociologists but students who have passed an examination called 'Sociology'! The unintended consequence of the examination system seems to be that students who know facts about sociologists are more successful than those who understand what sociology is all about.

Equally so, in subjects like History, students learn historical facts rather than how to do History. For example, the JMB 'A' level History syllabuses offer an optional question on documents, together with a compulsory one, asking candidates to attempt some understanding of the material and its background. However, the option question refers to 'seen' documents which might allow students to answer the question without actually understanding the process of document analysis, of doing History.

What we would like to be doing in the classroom is obviously related to our view of sociology as a discipline. We see sociology as a 'doing' subject rather than a 'reading about what other people called sociologists have written or done' subject. The essence of sociology is the sociological imagination, and we are concerned with encouraging its development in our students. We take as our starting point C. Wright Mills' understanding of sociology as a discipline which makes a link between the 'personal troubles of milieu' and the 'public issues of social structure'. For example, when an individual is unemployed that is personal trouble. When that person is one of 3.5 million unemployed it is also a public issue, and their unemployment is not a consequence of some individual failing but rather of some feature of the structure of society. C. Wright Mills points out that recognising this relationship is central to having sociological understanding.

> To be aware of the idea of social structure and to use it with sensibility is to be capable of tracing such linkages among a variety of milieux. To be able to do that is to possess the sociological imagination. (C.Wright Mills, 1970, p.17).

As such, then, the sociological imagination is about self-consciousness, an understanding of one's position in society and how that society directs, constrains and presents possibilities for action. Our concern as teachers with the flowering of the sociological imagination is that it is central to our role and in classroom

197

practice we seek to translate that concern into a teaching objective of developing sociological skills.
We are concerned to develop the type of skills which enable students to see the relationship between those sorts of things that are covered in a theoretical way in class and their everyday uses. We are attempting to get our students to begin to make sense of what happens to them - at school, at work, wherever, in some sociological way. That is why many of the CEE projects which we refer to later concern the daily lives of the students who undertake them. Examples are: 'The reaction of customers in a well-known supermarket to rudeness from myself, a part-time stocklad'; 'The relevance of social class in a casual encounter at the train station'; 'Observation of a group's reaction to unconventional dress on someone who has always been known to dress conventionally'; 'Monotony at work and how it is overcome'; and 'A challenge to preconceived ideas - the lodger game'.

We are not concerned solely with the preparation of students for examinations called sociology, but in developing a sociological outlook which recognises that the individual exists in relation to others as a part of society.

The problem is, though, that to pursue such an approach gets in the way of examination preparation. The demands of the 'A' level system, are such that there is little time or place for the encouragement of personal reflection on one's social life. The 'A' levels are not concerned so much <u>with</u> sociology as with little packets of information <u>about</u> sociology, other people's sociology. It is <u>also</u> an unreal abstract sociology in that there is little room for people. In 'A' level examination sociology no-one ever gets socialised, labelled or selected, these are processes to write about, not to understand as personal experiences. Personal anecdotal evidence, the value of which has been questioned by Her Majesty's Inspectorate (HMI 1983a, p.7 and 1983b, p.35), has no place in official examination sociology. Consequently, 'A' level examination sociology is an arid sociology. However, as the work of our CEE students reveals, personal anecdotes, can display a wealth of sociological imagination.

EXAMINATIONS AND TEACHING

The popular image of 'A' level Sociology is that it is a soft option. One of the consequences of this view is that 'A' level sociology students have a lower level of achievement in terms of average number of 'O' level passes than the average for all students on 'A' level courses. This is not a problem which pertains to sociology alone. Advanced Level Design, for example, has a low status within the academic structure, as do subjects like Home Economics and Fashion and Fabrics. Students who are not considered 'bright' enough for traditional 'A' level subjects are 'allowed' to take take courses in these low status subjects. We suggest, however, that the degree of intellectual sophistication required to tackle a problem solving course like 'A' level Design, with its considerable cross-curricular activities, makes Design difficult rather than easy. Similarly the 'easy' label ascribed to sociology is not congruent with the students' own views of their own particular experiences. Indeed, it appears that the examining boards themselves have in mind an 'ideal' 'A' level candidate who is capable of handling sophisticated theoretical concepts and detailed empirical analyses at the same time, whilst also being able to assess the internal and external strengths and weaknesses of such concepts and examples within one or more sociological perspectives (and all within a 45 minute essay). This is, we believe, considerably more than is expected of candidates sitting 'A' level examinations in many other subjects. The level of skills, knowledge and understanding required for the satisfactory completion of such a daunting task should merit the label 'extremely difficult' rather than 'easy'.

Does all this mean that 'A' level sociology examinations have gone too far, or that the task has become so daunting that it is impossible for the 'average' eighteen year old candidate? The level of popularity of 'A' level sociology would seem to indicate that this is not necessarily the case. Furthermore, statistics concerning success rates seem to back up this point. In 1983, for example, 18,379 students sat 'A' level sociology examinations organised by six examining boards; and between 1981 and 1983 there was a 15 per cent increase in the number of candidates. Statistics from the AEB, with the largest entry in 1983 of 13,923, point to a success rate of 51.7 per cent (McNeill, 1984, p.57). There is evidence that candidates from sixth form colleges achieve success rates of over 70 per cent. Such figures could hardly be presented as evidence that sociology 'A' level is too difficult. So what is happening to 'A' level classes to achieve such high success rates in the face of the apparent impossibility of the task?

We believe the answer to this question is that the sociology teachers who achieve these levels of success have 'sussed out' the examination system. Sociology 'A' level is not such a 'hit-and-miss' affair because, with experience, it is possible to 'uncover' exactly what a Chief Examiner expects and teach students to fulfil his expectations. There is a vast difference between the study of sociology and the study of 'A' level sociology for examination success.

The major reason for this position is the formulation of the majority of present 'A' level syllabuses, but a syllabus only becomes meaningful in an examination context. It is the expectations of the 'A' level examiners which determine what is taught in 'A' level classes. They define what is 'good' or 'bad' sociology. This influence is now so strong, especially when taken in conjunction with the desires of Principals and Headteachers for statistics which 'prove' that successful teaching is taking place, that is it necessary to teach for examination success rather than guiding students towards an appreciation of the value of sociology as a method of inquiry. Time is so short in 'A' level courses that teachers are forced into being highly selective. The extension of the AEB syllabus in 1982 to include three new topic areas - the Sociology of Knowledge, Health and Medicine and Development - increases the need for this selectivity. Furthermore, the publication recently of several textbooks designed to answer the needs of current 'A' level syllabuses means that the selection is already made for the teacher. It is no longer necessary for students to read 'original' sociological texts, so long as they know a 'potted version' of them.

We appreciate that these concerns are not new. Gribble (1969, p.63, his italics) for example, points out that 'there can be no valid distinction....between teaching, say, history as a "body of knowledge" and teaching history as an "activity". If it is history that is being taught, i.e. that form of knowledge called history, then both the procedures of inquiry and the body of knowledge must be passed on'. Similarly, Barnes and Barnes, (1983, p.34), in an analysis of the teaching of English in Colleges of Further Education point out how various constraints, including 'the tightness or looseness of examination requirements' can affect students' experiences of the curriculum. We would like to illustrate the

nature of these constraints by referring to our own
teaching of sociology in a sixth form college, to
try to make sense of our experiences and to try to
understand how examination requirements fit into the
mechanisms which organise knowledge within schools
and classrooms. These experiences are matched by
other teachers of other subjects in other institutions. By concentrating on how this process might
work in sociology teaching, we do not wish to imply
that the process does not work in this way in
other contexts.

LANGUAGE AND SOCIOLOGY

In all there are eight sociology classes in the
sixth form college where we work. Five of these
follow Advanced Level courses (AEB), one follows
an Ordinary level course (AEB) and two follow Mode
III Certificate of Extended Education (CEE) Courses,
one in Sociology and one in Social Studies (ALSEB)
both of which are assessed by means of course work
with no formal examination. It is our contention
that the freedom which a non-examination course
offers allows students to develop a sociological
imagination without having to package it in a
certain phraseology for examiners' consumption.
Furthermore, that in being concerned to get the
phraseology correct, teachers are in danger of
forgetting the underlying sociological principles.
    In this piece of classroom research we have
tried to identify the main strands of the problems
which face students so that we might establish the
nature of the problems and also consider whether
it is possible to overcome them.   These issues
we might call 'the problem of language', and 'the
problem of concepts'.
    By the 'problem of language' we are interested
in whether the nature of the examination syllabus
at 'A' level, which places certain expectation
on the students in terms of the ways in which they
should describe and explain sociological concept
is so constricting that it prevents the 'flowering
of the sociological imagination'. Obviously
contained within this problem is the extent to
which the teacher imposes his definition of the
situation. As teachers it became apparent to us
that we might be in danger of denying our students
access to the 'correct answer' because they failed
to use the appropriate language. This may, if it
was happening, lead to a loss of confidence on the
part of the student and therefore have undesirable

consequences in other areas of their study of
sociology.

Thus we have a clearly defined problem; the
difficult issue is 'how has it developed'?

With regard to the 'problem of language' an
examination of transcripts of 'A' level classes
demonstrates that perfectly reasonable sociology
is being rejected by the teacher because the 'wrong'
or inappropriate language is being used. In order
that we might establish whether it is the teacher or
the constraints of the examination which is responsible for this we intend to examine two different
levels of sociology class, CEE Sociology and 'A'
level Sociology, so that we can compare our activities as teachers. We feel that the advantage of this
form of comparison is that the CEE classes are Mode
III continual assessment courses involving no written
examination, thus we can compare 'non-examination'
course with examination courses of different levels
and different linguistic expectations. In this way
we should be able to establish whether as teachers
we can teach sociology within a non-'A' level context.

Extract One - Advanced Level Class

Teacher: What is it that we have to be able
            to make a connection with when we
            are talking about methodology?
            Sociological methods do not exist
            on their own....they are part of the
            relationship between methodology and
            what?

Student 1: We have to know what we are talking
            about

Teacher: What is a better way of saying that?

Student 2: Perspectives!

Teacher: Or Theory There is a very strong
            relationship between theory and
            methods..... remember

Extract Two - Advanced Level Class

Teacher: What might happen if an observer
            becomes too interested in the group
            of people he is observing or the
            focus of his research.

202

Student 3:   It might alter his point of view

Teacher: Or as we sociologists would say....
he might lose his objectivity.

Extract Three - CEE Class

Teacher: What happens when an observer gets
too involved with the group he is
observing?

Student 4:   He will probably forget that he is
a sociologist like and just join in
what we do.

Teacher: Good - that's what might happen.

These extracts clearly illustrate the point made
earlier about our ability to define certain answers
as correct. What was wrong with the contributions
of S1 and S2 in Extract One? What is better about
the word 'theory'? This word may be more acceptable
from the examiner's point of view than 'perspectives',
but does it really mean any more from a student's
point of view than what S1 and S2 said? Furthermore,
does it add to their understanding? Equally so,
in Extract Two: did S3 really mean what the teacher
took it to mean, or did she have something else in
mind? Here the teacher jumps in to impose his
interpretation of the statement by S3, but in a way
that points out to S3 and the rest of the group what
is the 'correct' way of answering the question.
However, in Extract Three, the teacher 'knowing' that
in the context of a CEE class there is no need to use
the correct language, accepts what S4 says without
attempting to alter the phraseology. The point at
issue here is whether what S3 and S4 said is the same
or different, and is it correct? We would argue that
S3 and S4 are both saying the same thing and that
they are both correct in sociological terms. However,
within the classroom context S3 is defined as incorrect
because of the fact that she is taking an 'A' level
examination which the teacher has interpreted as
demanding a certain sort of phraseology. What is of
more concern to the teacher is not whether S3 is right
or not, but that she and the other students learn
the correct word.

The 'problem of concepts' arises because of the
abstract nature of sociology. Empirical or

impressionistic analyses are valuable but they
do not explain the fundamental dynamic of the
nature of the construction, maintenance and re-
construction of social order. Consequently,
abstractions which do not exist in the real world
have to be made so that reality can be approached.
Sociology is full of 'higher level concepts' which
define problems and show how 'lower level concepts'
or more specific concepts fit within a general
framework. Perhaps one of the most important higher
level concepts is the nature of sociological 'work'
itself. This problem is illustrated by our students
not being able to recognise when sociological work
is taking place.

Sometimes though, class activities do get to
grips with what we have identified as real sociology.
Given the nature of the topics to be covered this
is probably inevitable. In one particular 'A' level
lesson the discussion centred around 'how others
see us'. This focussed on judgements in school,
and led to a consideration of the role and behaviour
of teachers. It was noted that teachers are expected
to behave in some vaguely defined way, and that the
definition may vary from establishment to establishment.   In particular, different types of school may
operate different types of definition - public or
state schools, primary or secondary schools for
example. So we began to list the ways in which
teachers in our college acted in a different fashion
to the teachers in the 11-16 schools the students
had previously attended. The conclusions were that
teachers at our college were:
>   less concerned with social control;
>   more concerned as subject specialists;
>   on a softer option because they taught fewer
>   students;
>   subject to more examination pressures;
>   more likely to acknowledge the students in
>   corridors.

We began to develop some explanations for these
differences, applying the theoretical knowledge
gleaned from earlier lessons. In our college,
teachers acknowledge students in corridors not
because we are a friendlier bunch, but because we
have fewer students to say 'hello' to. The
responsibility for social control is, in part,
devolved to the individual student, who has
'volunteered' for extra schooling. There is no
commitment on the part of the college: if a
customer is awkward enough he will be 'cooled
out' or asked to leave.

The differences in teachers' behaviour were explained and understood in terms of differences in the structures of schools and sixth form colleges. The students, by discussing the differences, were able to develop an understanding of teachers' behaviour in terms of different constraints and different possibilities. As they had made use of their developing sociological imagination, the lesson could well be defined as a success, a good lesson, by the teacher. But the students did not recognise this particular lesson, or others like it, as 'work'. Work is to do with writing things down, reading books, writing essays, preparing for examinations. Because this lesson did not involve putting pen to paper, but was based on talking, speculation, anecdotes and making occasional witty comments about teachers' behaviour, it was a 'good' lesson because it <u>avoided</u> work. It was an amusing, interesting diversion in an otherwise tedious day, in an otherwise tedious subject, just like the rest.

This gap between our interpretation of the lesson and the students' interpretation is central to the 'problem of concepts'. As we said earlier, one of the higher concepts we are concerned with is the nature of doing sociological work. This lesson illustrated for us the students' ability to do exactly what C. Wright Mills talks about, to make those linkages, to <u>do</u> sociology. The students do not, however, recognise such a lesson as work; they also fail, therefore, to recognise it as sociology, because the two are equated - sociology means work. Sociology is not about them and their teachers, it concerns essays about teachers and pupils who only exist in an abstract examination sociology world. Thus, when we feel we are being successful in developing a sociological approach, the students feel that they are being successful in getting us off the point, as they see it. They are, because of the restriction of the examination, unable to recognise what sociology is. They fail to see that sociology is about themselves and their lives, as a part of society and its history. The unintended consequences of examinations work in two directions, on the teachers and on the pupils and act as a double bind, not only in sociology but in many subjects.

We see our role as sociology teachers as consisting of three elements: preparing students for some examinations called 'sociology'; developing an interest in the discipline; and nurturing a critical and questioning approach to problems, evidence and people with axes to grind. This three part role

contains, in our opinion, a tension between the
examination element and those elements which are
more educative, in a wider sense. This feeling is
not unique to us nor to other teachers; the com-
plaint or worry that the remoteness of the examination process causes syllabuses and examinations to
present barriers to the 'real' nature of the
subject will be echoed by many other teachers, at
all levels of the examination system. We find it
to be a particular problem, though, because inevitabl
it causes a parallel tension or conflict for our
students.
    Sociology is like other subjects in leading to
the same sort of examinations. It could be different
if we decided that sociology came first, but it is no
as the students' main interest is, understandably,
examination success. Thus there is a conflict on the
one hand between what we would like to do and what
the students are initially expecting and on the other
hand, what the examination means we must do. Therefore one of the unintended consequences of examinations is to make sociology courses unsociological.

SOCIOLOGY IN ACTION

What we feel is required are courses which emphasise
the putting into practice of concepts and methods,
rather than reading and writing about concepts and
methods as used by someone else. This means courses
with opportunities for student research and project
work. Within the current 'A' level structures there
is little incentive for a student's own research
investigations because there is no way for it to be
assessed directly and because it is very difficult,
given the type of questions set, for students to
utilise self-generated knowledge. In fact, the
expansion of the AEB 'A' level sociology syllabus in
1982 saw at the same time the demise of the project
option and question on Paper Two.
    We know that students of this age can carry out
small scale research exercises because we do so
with our CEE classes. The courses are course-work
assessed, and are explicitly doing courses with
sixty per cent of the marks allocated to work
directed by the students. They do their own media
analysis, visit courts and design, administer and
analyse questionnaires. In particular at the end
of the one year course they undertake a research
project which accounts for twenty per cent of the
marks available. This project is an investigation
by the students. It is not a reading project,

requiring them to send away for leaflets to be copied
out, as so much of the work at this level is.   Rather
the project involves the students;   they find out for
themselves about some social situation of which they
are a part or to which they have access.   Their
investigation may be based on observations, interviews or questionnaires or a combination of these
methods, whichever is appropriate.

Much of the work produced is of a very high
quality, demonstrating the students' understanding
of sociology, their 'feel' for the sociological
imagination and their critical awareness of what
has been studied.   As the following extracts show,
it is possible for 17 year olds to produce good
sociology.   It should be noted, too, that these are
not 'A' level students, but CEE students who, at the
end of the fifth year in secondary school, have poor
academic backgrounds.   The point about the sociological imagination is that is it accessible to almost
everybody.   It is not something which entails a technical vocabulary, because it is basically exercising
the recognition that the events which occur in
society have some consequence for the individual,
and understanding how individual lives are affected
by the structures of that society.

Extract Four

This extract comes from a project entitled
'A Study of Reactions to the Disruption of
Reality'.   In order to conduct the survey
the girl involved deliberately confused the name
of her fiancé with that of his identical twin.

Pat: Come in Ken.

Steve: Hey! What do you mean, Ken!

Pat: Well that's your name, fool!

Steve: No it's not and you know it.

Pat: Oh, shut up and sit down in the front
           room.

((By this time I had told my mam what I was doing
and she agreed to help me.))

Mam: Hi Ken. Do you want a cup of tea?

Steve: Now come on, what's all this? Is it a
           joke?'

((Steve did not understand and was already
showing signs of confusion......))

((They move to have a meal))

Steve: Pass on the sauce, please.

((I passed him the red, imagining his reaction))

Steve: You've passed me the wrong sauce Pat.

Pat: No I haven't, it's the one you always
         have.

Steve: It's Ken who likes red sauce, not me.

Pat: Don't be silly you're Ken. Are you
         trying to get me annoyed again?

Steve: No! Oh Pat, you're beginning to confuse
         me.

Pat: Oh really Ken, just carry on eating your
         tea. For goodness sakes stop this
         nonsense.......

Conclusion

During this time I had spent pretending that
my boy friend Steve was Ken I noticed that
his feelings had changed, his charming attitudes
had vanished. When near him, he made me feel
cold and outcasted. No relationship was shown
between us. A general kiss became hard to get
and holding hands was out of the question.
I have proved to myself that....when challenging
the 'real thing' it can cause upset and anger.
This is because the communication balance has
been tampered with.....I have found that people
do have a fixed reaction to reality and are not
able to adapt to it quickly. Also that those
who want to play need to understand what goes
on. But in everyday life it is not always clear
what the rules and goals are, or what behaviour
is acceptable.

This extract illustrates that Pat has uncovered for
herself the nature of power in relationships to define
the situation, the importance of rule governed behaviour, the nature of symbolic gestures (red sauce)
and the problems of not understanding what is going

on. This is a typical example of many of this type
of project which CEE students conduct each year and
shows the flowering of the sociological imagination.

Extract Five

The next extract comes from a project about
'shoplifting'. We appreciate that it might
confirm everybody's worst fears about sociologists and sociology teaching. However, the
treatment of social problems like crime is an
important issue and at the same time problematic. Consequently, when the students involved
asked if they could undertake the project they
explained that it was the suggestion of the
manager of a store where one of the students
worked for whom shoplifting was not a sociological problem but a practical one. The
students, therefore, set out to try to establish
if customers could be utilised in the store
manager's fight against shoplifting. Furthermore, as the extract itself shows, this piece
of work clearly illustrates the advantages
of experiential learning.

The project was entitled 'Analysis of Shoplifting'. In it two students wished to
establish whether or not what people thought
they would do when seeing a shoplifter matched
reality. To this end they devised a research
programme which involved asking customers
outside a shop what they would do if they saw
a shoplifter. One student actually did the
'shoplifting' in front of the people already
questioned; the other observed their reactions.
In order to add more sophistication to the
situation the 'shoplifter' was dressed for
part of the experience in 'dirty, scruffy
clothes' and for another part in 'standard
smart dress'. The analysis of the result was
presented according to age groups. For example:

From doing this and experiencing being caught
I found people differed greatly when they were
just talking about it to seeing it in real
life.

Whereas the under 21s on average say they
would turn a blind eye and would not consider

it important they totally changed their
views in real life as, depending on their
size, they would either hold you on the spot
and discuss it and then report you. Girls
were more encouraging, lads would take most
action....

In the age group 50 to 65 their views changed
drastically and this age group had the highest
percentage of males. They would approach you
like some kind of army sergeant or policeman
with plenty of authority and first of all give
you an inferiority complex followed by a lecture.
For example, one said he did not fight at Dunkirk
to have 'riff raff like you behaving like this.
You should be working to get yourself out of the
gutter'. (This was when I was dressed in shabby
dirty clothing). He showed a substantial amount
of prejudice to me and really seemed to be looking for attention from anyone who was passing.
He seemed to be upper class. Whereas the wives
of this type of men seemed to hide behind them.
On their own they may well have turned a blind
eye, which none of them said they would do in
the questionnaire.

We found that people were strongly influenced
by the way people dressed, yet when they were
asked if they would be prejudiced against people
who may appear to be from a lower class background they predominantly said 'no', showing
great sympathy for these people. In real life
I found that when I changed into shabby clothes
I was treated with less respect by most people.
When dressed shabbily we were not once approached with sympathy or given advice to stop as we
were when we were in good clothing.

In this project the students involved demonstrated
a fairly sophisticated understanding of what is
probably a very basic but often ignored truth.
People do not always say what they mean. In this
way they uncovered for themselves one of the basic
problems of questionnaire analyses and the weaknesses of the sorts of sociological theories which
depend upon questionnaires for data. Furthermore,
they uncovered for themselves the importance of symbo
(dress) in everyday life, and the way in which social
stratification (by age, class and gender) can influence the outcome of social situations. Both
extracts four and five are typical CEE projects

conducted by students who, on average, have no
greater than CSE grade 2 results prior to commencing
the course.

What these extracts show mostly is that learning
by doing not only can but does go on. A well formulated and conducted piece of research can yield
both worthwhile information and an understanding of
methodological issues. Research allows students to
begin to make sense of some part of the social
world by applying to it concepts learned in the
classroom. This process of application is a rein-
forcing and fixing process. This is not a process
which is new or radical, not is it exclusive to
sociology. As one geography 'A' level student
said, 'When I was learning about soils in the
classroom they didn't really mean very much to me -
but now that I have spent a day digging them up I can
begin to see the relationships between different
types of soils, I can begin to understand them'. But
for sociology students the benefits may be even
greater. Research techniques themselves are
inextricably linked to a particular set of sociological theories and performing the research task can
illuminate not only the 'worthwhile information'
and the problems of particular research techniques
but also they assist the learning of sociological
theory. Sociological research illuminates the
nature of sociological work, it necessitates students
developing a sociological imagination. Consequently,
sociological research helps to overcome the bigger
problem we have outlined above, the 'problem of
concepts'.

CONCLUSION

It is interesting to note that during the period when
research projects have become an important part of
the course in 'A' level Geography (eg the JMB Syllabus
B), the AEB has dropped from its 'A' level Sociology
syllabus the project option causing the subject to
become even more a course in 'learning about what other
people have done'. Perhaps the reasoning behind the
AEB's decision was legitimate because less then one
per cent of candidates attempted this question. But
possibly the solution was not to withdraw the option
but to remove it from the question paper itself and
make it more like the JMB geography syllabus B system
with projects marked by teachers and then either
externally moderated or moderated through the examination scores. What we believe our classroom practice shows is that it is possible to develop a

sociological imagination by doing sociology. At present 'A' level syllabuses do not allow for that to happen. One possibility, however, has recently emerged. The introduction of a new JMB 'A' level syllabus in sociology to be tested for the first time in 1985.

The main thrust of this syllabus is not a list of 'sociology of......' like the AEB. Instead students are helped to understand the nature of social stratification, social control and social change throug whatever substantive material the teacher finds suit-able. This new syllabus allows teachers much greater control over the sort of material he or she wishes to use and so might allow student research to be intro-duced. Realistically, however, syllabuses do not mean very much until they are translated into exam-ination questions. Although we will have to wait until June 1985 to see what sort of questions appear, the specimen questions published so far do not really allow students to develop answers based on their own doing of sociology. It may well be that the new JMB syllabus will have the same unintended consequences that we hoped it might remove, i.e. the teaching of sociology will not develop a method of understanding, but rather will impart skills of passing examinations.

The implication of this analysis of our sociology teaching and ourselves as teachers is that examina-tions can obstruct learning. We are not suggesting that examinations are wholly bad. They are an integra element of the process of curriculum development. Chief Examiners reports and changes in the style and content of examination syllabuses and question papers cause teachers to change their ideas about what to teach and how to teach it from time to time. However, we feel that examinations should be more flexible. They should allow students to benefit from experientia learning rather than stifling the development of such learning. Furthermore self-generated material is more open to self-criticism. Students themselves know when they have cut corners. Self-criticism is a sign of maturity, a quality which the education process ought to encourage. What we need is an examination system which allows us to do this. Unfortunately 'knowing that' still appears to be more important than 'knowing how' and so there is a mismatch between the style of learning required for examination purposes and that which is required for individual experiential work. However, if what students learn in school is to be beneficial to them as adults then 'knowing how' will have to become more important. If, as we have suggested, examinations themselves are partly

212

responsible for teaching styles then in order to
bring about a shift in emphasis within the classroom
examinations themselves will have to change.

REFERENCES

Barnes, D., and Barnes, D., (1983),'Preparing to
    Write in Further Education'in Hammersley, M.,
    and Hargreaves, A., (eds), Curriculum Practice:
    Some Sociological Case Studies, The Falmer Press
    Lewes, Sussex.
Gribble, B., (1969), Introduction to Philosophy of
    Education, Allyn and Bacon Inc., Boston, USA.
HMI (1983a) 'O' Level Sociology in some Schools and
    Colleges.
HMI (1983b) Report by HM Inspector on Esher College,
    Surrey.
McNeill, P., (1984),'GCE Sociology. Entries and
    Grades Awarded 1983',The Social Science Teacher,
    Vol 13, No.2, Spring,pp 56-57.
Wright Mills, C., (1970), The Sociological Imagination,
    Penguin Books, Harmondsworth.

Chapter Eleven

UNDERSTANDING STUDENTS: TEACHERS' PROBLEMS OF
ASSESSMENT

Harry Osser

This chapter begins with an analysis of the critical
differences between psychometric and clinical assessment practices with respect to their goals, assumptions and procedures.   Then the topics of the complex nature of teacher judgement of students, and
of observation as one type of clinical assessment,
will be discussed.   The argument continues with an
examination of the several forms of knowledge that
students employ in the course of their school performances and it concludes with an extended illustration of the use of clinical assessment in understanding students' knowledge and attitudes.

PSYCHOMETRIC AND CLINICAL ASSESSMENTS

Psychometric tests may be given to an individual or
a group of students.   Typically, the intention of
the tester is to capture the <u>product</u> of learning,
in order to answer the question, 'What proportion
of the school curriculum has been <u>learned</u> by this
student, or these students?'   The accepted procedure is for the tester to offer a standardised
sequence of questions to those being assessed.
The results of psychometric testing provide global
information such as: 'The student has an IQ of 'X',
is reading at a 'Y' level, and is working at the
'Z' level in mathematics'.   This information may be
used to allocate a student to a particular group, or
sub-group, in school.
        In contrast, clinical assessments are indiv-
idualised, both with respect to the one-to-one relationship between tester and student as well as to
the form and content of the questions presented in
the testing situation.   Clinical assessment focusses
on the question, 'What does this student know?' and
is not restricted to what has been learned from the

214

school curriculum. The shift in emphasis is from the identification of the products of school learning to the exploration of the <u>processes</u> involved in the generation of these products. The potential benefits of a clinical assessment include the provision of information about the individual student's difficulties with specific features of school work, such as failure to adhere to an appropriate sequence of 'moves' in solving a mathematical problem. In other words, clinical tests are characteristically diagnostic, and refer to the variety of kinds of learning the student engages in.

The psychometric and clinical methods of assessment are related to distinctly different conceptual territories, so that beyond the obvious differences in means of assessment, there are also differences in goals. Underlying such differences are divergent preconceptions of the actual nature of students' school learning. Psychometric testing rests upon a mechanical theory which essentially represents the students simply as passive absorbers of lessons. This view results quite naturally in a testing instrument designed to measure the extent to which they are able to <u>reproduce the content of lessons</u>. On the other hand, clinical testing stems from a theoretical position which emphasises the autonomous character of their cognitive life. From this perspective, students are seen as being <u>actively</u> engaged in organising reality. The procedures used in clinical testing therefore represent attempts to discover how they are structuring, and restructuring, their school experiences, and what forms their knowledge takes.

The selection of a particular test procedure depends upon the nature of the judgement that has to be made. If initial screening is necessary to select the type of level of classroom for a student, a psychometric test might well be appropriate; such testing however will only provide information for classifying the student. If it is necessary to go beyond simple classification in order, for instance, to reveal, in a significant manner, details of particular problems in responding to school work, clinical assessment procedures might be considered. Anyone who has attempted to make cognitive processes explicit realises that a variety of difficulties will be encountered in electing to use such a strategy. Yet the challenge must be taken up, as Rowntree (1977) puts it, 'Rather than making the measureable important, we should make the important measureable'. (p.68).

THE COMPLEXITY AND LIMITATIONS OF TEACHERS' OBSERVATION OF STUDENTS

One of the common myths in education is that teachers have detailed knowledge of what parts of the curriculum individual students have mastered, what interests each possesses, what pleases and distresses them, and finally which teaching strategy must be used to harness their full intellectual and motivational resources in the processes of learning. This kind of extensive knowledge of the strengths and weaknesses of individual students is rare. One of the main reasons for this is that the basic question in evaluation, namely 'What does this student know?', while appearing at first to be simple, turns out on analysis to be of considerable complexity. Answers to this question may be pursued in a number of different ways, including looking at students in classrooms. However, for observation to lead to a proper understanding of classroom events it is necessary to go beyond simple description. As Walker and Adelman (1975, p.18), put it, 'The essence of observation is the creation of insight out of what might seem initially to be routine and commonplace'.

What often results from asking a teacher to describe a particular student is the provision of a verbal sketch which includes such words as attentive, bored, underachiever, overachiever, slow learner, gifted, passive, hyperactive, clumsy, or well-coordinated. This list of descriptions represents only a small part of the total lexicon of educators. The function of these terms, or labels, is to permit the teacher to organise observational experience. Given that the number of adjectives typically available to an educated adult is very large, a pressing question is 'How does a teacher select specific terms in characterising the school performance of a particular student?'

The argument so far is that teachers have sources of information about students, including observational data, out of which they develop a category scheme, consisting of a set of verbal descriptions, which they use to sort their students into various functional groups. Another basic question here is, 'What particular kinds of information are critical constituents of the teacher's judgement?' To use a concrete example, how does a teacher come to characterise a student as, for example, a 'good' reader? This judgement presumably derives from the teacher's observation that the

student has most, or all, of the defining attributes of a good reader. Such a judgement derives
from the teacher's possibly implicit theory of reading. One teacher, for example, might view a 'good'
reader as somebody who is flawless in pronouncing
words gone over in a lesson. Another teacher might
insist that the student be able to read 'new' words,
for which no instructions have been directly given,
before applying the label 'good' reader.

Different performances in reading by two
students may be judged to be the same by several
teachers, or the same performance may be judged
differently by these teachers. Furthermore, the same
general cue may have a variety of meanings for any
given teacher. For example the raised hand is a culturally accepted signal indicating that the attention of
the teacher is being sought. But as Walker and
Adelman (1975, p.3) point out, 'The raised hand is
not just a signal of application to speak; for the
style in which it is performed can be used to
communicate a whole range of feelings about the
teacher, the lesson, the time of day, or other
children'. The teacher has to <u>interpret</u> the cue
by moving from its general meaning to the unique
meaning given in the context of observation. The
following example of a signal with multiple meanings
illustrates this point:

> During World War II, I became at first
> bemused, and later intrigued by the
> repertoire of meanings which could be
> drawn upon an experienced United States
> Army private and transmitted to accom-
> paniment to a hand salute. The salute,
> a conventionalized movement of the right
> hand to the vicinity of the anterior portion
> of the cap or hat, could, without occasioning
> a court martial, be performed in a manner
> which could satisfy, please, or enrage the
> most demanding officer. By shifts in
> stance, facial expression, the velocity
> or duration of the movement of salutation,
> and even in the selection of inappropriate
> contexts from the act, the soldier could
> dignify, ridicule, demean, seduce, insult,
> or promote the recipient of the salute....
> I once watched a sergeant give a 3-second,
> brilliant criticism of English cooking in
> an elaborate inverted salute to a beef-and-
> kidney-pie.
> (Birdwhistell, 1970, pp 79-80).

217

To return to the classroom example, some of the
students who do not know the answer to the teacher's
question may nevertheless still raise their hands,
so the teacher's task is to see through this bluff
by integrating past knowledge of these students with
a quick reading of available cues.

Another common dilemma for teachers concerns
judging the attentiveness of students. How does the
teacher know if they are paying attention? If they
are quiet? If they are looking at the teacher? If
they look 'interested'? If they ask questions?
Notwithstanding the fact that many of the cues available for scrutiny in the classroom are 'fluid, fluc-
tuating, transient and fragile'. (Walker and Adelman,
1975, p.25). many of the teachers' judgements are
accurate, even though they must be made very rapidly
and under difficult circumstances. For instance,
in judging a single student, the teacher has to
attend to many events, each of which varies in tempo,
intensity, and meaningfulness. An analogy might
be with the array of cues involved in the judgement
of a gymnast's performance. However, as knowledge
is gained of the student, the teacher begins to
sample more efficiently from among the available
cues in assessing the student.

THE TEACHER AS OBSERVER: IMPLICATIONS FOR STUDENT
EVALUATION

It has been argued that a teacher develops a categorical scheme concerning student performance which
helps in developing a profile of the strengths and
weaknesses of any one student. Such a categorical
scheme intersects with a teacher's implicit psycho-
educational theories, and both place constraints on
observation and evaluation. According to this
viewpoint, observation is never pure and direct,
but is instead filtered through the teacher's
theories. These may take the form, for example,
of beliefs that students from a particular family,
or of a certain age, sex, race, or social class are
capable (or incapable) of specific forms of academic
development. Consider, for example, the real case
of a boy who had been labelled a nonreader at 8
years of age. His teachers were pleased that under
their guidance he had developed after four months
of the new school year to the point where he could
read simple books to them. They now judged him to
be one year behind his classmates. In fact,
through independent testing, it was discovered to
the teachers' surprise, or even dismay, that the

boy was now among the best in the class. His teachers' underlying assumption seems to have been that
for a nonreader the most that one can reasonably
expect, even with skilled teaching, is a small amount
of progress in several months. This is an instance
in which a theoretical viewpoint limited the teachers'
evaluation, in fact resulting in a mis-evaluation of
the student.

To answer the question, 'What does this student
know?' in any complete sense clearly demands <u>more</u>
than simple observation. Consider these three
examples of a student's performance in elementary
mathematics:

Student's Work	Teacher's Judgement	Alternate Interpretation
$\begin{array}{r} 119 \\ +200 \\ \hline 319 \end{array}$	Correct	Correct answer but poor strategy as student added from the left.
$\begin{array}{r} 329 \\ +852 \\ \hline 11711 \end{array}$	Incorrect	Same strategy resulting in a wrong solution.
$\begin{array}{r} 19 \\ 89 \\ 17 \\ +16 \\ \hline 123 \end{array}$	Incorrect	Righthand column added correctly but total of 31 was reversed, the student carried the 1.

These examples suggest that the mere observation of
the end products of the student's work cannot, by
itself, provide the teacher with anything like an
adequate understanding of both <u>what</u> and <u>how</u> the
student is learning. What is required is the use
of procedures which permit the teacher to 'observe'
the student's learning processes. In these three
examples, the explication of the problem-solving
process was achieved by asking the student to say
out aloud what he was doing as he was working at the
problems. The next section provides an outline
account of student competence and also a detailed
illustration of how, by using clinical assessment
procedures, a teacher, or a researcher, can arrive
at useful conclusions about the strategies students
use as they engage in school mathematics.

THE CONSTITUENTS OF SCHOOL KNOWLEDGE

In considering what the individual in the role of
student has to know to be successful, an account of
school work expressed solely in terms of his necessary grasp of the formal units of the curriculum would
be inadequate: the student is equally exposed to a
latent and informal curriculum of school values.
One approach to the exploration of the character
of school success is to determine the critical
competencies that the student has to develop, and
use, in order to cope with the demands of school.
For example, Mehan (1980) has proposed that in order
to participate effectively in the classroom students
need to synchronise two forms of knowledge, one
covering academic content, the other interactional
form. In other words, it is not enough to have
mastered the content of a subject-matter, they must
also be sensitive to the classroom rules that govern
the presentation of such knowledge. Mehan's discussion on the nature of school knowledge is reformulated in the next section.

In developing a conceptual framework to make
sense out of school experience, students, it will
be argued, operate simultaneously with three kinds
of knowledge. The first type is <u>academic knowledge</u>,
or grasp of the content of subject-matter (Osser,1980)
The second is <u>social-cognitive knowledge</u> which refers
to the student's ability to both make meanings and
intentions clear to others, and to understand their
meanings and intentions (Osser,1982). As Erickson
and Shultz (1981,p.147) suggest:

> The production of appropriate social
> behaviour from moment to moment requires
> knowing what context one is in, and when
> contexts change, as well as knowing what
> behaviour is considered appropriate in
> these contexts.

The third kind, <u>metacognitive knowledge</u>, relates to
the student's skill in self-monitoring, illustrated
by the use of feedback and the resultant corrective
procedures. One linguistic example is the phenomenon of the 'retraced false start', where the
speaker detects a speech 'error' and corrects it by
the substitution, deletion, or addition of new
verbal materials (MacWhinney and Osser,1977). Other
equally common examples are where the student might
monitor task comprehension by asking such questions
as, 'What is this all about?' 'Is it difficult?'

'What is the next step?' and 'Did I forget
anything?'

A CLINICAL ASSESSMENT OF STUDENTS' METACOGNITIVE KNOWLEDGE

The following is an account of information generated
by a study of a teacher and her students in a special
class for children with substantial learning problems. One goal of the study was to analyse the role
of different types of knowledge in children's math-
matical performances. The following discussion will
focus on metacognitive knowledge. The skills of
meta cognition in mathematical problem-solving
include, for example, predicting, estimating and
checking, that is they refer to the basic characteristics of thinking efficiently in learning situations
(Flavell, 1979; Brown, 1980). A second goal was to
provide some information on the extent of the
teacher's influence on students' performances. For
example, they might on some occasions operate with
a 'formulaic' strategy in school learning where some,
or all, of the material would be memorised with
minimal understanding. On other occasions they
might adopt a 'generative' strategy, i.e. an attempt
to comprehend the relations between the elements of
a classroom task. The student using a formulaic
strategy may be voluntarily taking up, or be forced
into, a dependent learning role, simply acting as a
reproducer of the teacher's ideas, values, and
problem-solving strategies. Whereas the student
using the generative strategy is more likely to have
an independent learning role, and thus be an autonomous producer, or co-producer of knowledge with the
teacher.
    Clinical interviews of both the teacher and her
students were employed to discover the extent to
which students take up work strategies as previously
formulated by the teacher. In the following segment
of an interview with the teacher, the focus is on
the procedure of 'checking' as an instance of
monitoring school work. The interviewer speaks
first and the teacher describes how the students
are taught to check their work, and she comments
on their fidelity in following her recommendations.

    I: Do they check their work? Are they
          supposed to check their work?

    T: I have taught most of them how to
          check their own subtraction questions

by adding the bottom number with the answer to get the top one. Basically, it's just a visual check. 'Six divided by two. I have six put into groups of twos. I'm not going to get three, or twenty eight groups. I'm not going to get eighteen and I'm not going to get twelve. It doesn't make sense. I have to get a smaller number'. Just usually checking to make sure if it makes sense or not. 'If mother had five cookies and she gave four away, how many has she left? She can't possibly have nine'.

I: You were saying that they do this or they don't do this?

T: They're encouraged to do it.

I: And to what extent do they try to do that?

T: I don't think that many of them do it. They simply get their work done and hand it in and go on to something else. Get some free time or whatever have you. It's simply 'let's get it done'. There are some that try to get their work right but they won't check it to see if they have them right or have answered all the questions. This happens quite often. I'll call them back and say 'You didn't answer this question. You left that one out, you didn't do this one, what was the lesson? 'Oh, I didn't see those'. So they didn't go back to see if they had everything down. 'Did I have seven questions to copy off the board? Did I copy seven down? Did I copy five down?

I: So there's two kinds of checking that they are not always doing. One is just to see that you've completed the actual work, that you've put answers down or copied all the problems down that you were given. And the other is to see whether you've done the work properly, when you actually did it?

T: Right. If you allow them they just

222

don't do it. They think basically
'I've get to get my work done and
handed in, let the teacher check
it over. Then if I get the work
corrected, all right!.....'.

The teacher's assumptions seem to be that:

(1) The students typically do not check
to see whether they have copied all of
the work from the blackboard, or whether
they have answered every question.

(2) The students typically know appropriate
checking procedures which allow them to
arrive at an estimate of the right
answer, and thus can make progress
toward it.

(3) Nevertheless the students typically
leave it to her to check their work.

The following are samples from the interviews with
two female students, P_1 (Terry, 8 years) and P_2
(Carol, 11 years):

I: Do you ever check your work?

P_1: No, I try to, but I just make the
same math questions more worser,
so I just leave them alone.

I: Oh, what do you mean that you make
them worse?

P_1: Like if I hand 'em in and corrected
them, right? Then she says 'That one
certainly isn't that'. Say I handed
that in and it was ten hundred, and
she says 'That wasn't it'. I was
wrong.

I: Do you think sometimes you have them
right and then you change them when
you check?

P_1: Well, I never check no more because
I used to get them wrong. Now I sort
of get them wrong the same way.

223

I: Do you ever check your work?

P$_2$:   No I just look over it. Well when we're
       supposed to, like, um when Mrs W was here
       we, we um did this kind of thing and she
       would put the answers up on the board
       and we would check them by ourselves
       and that's fun 'cause I like doing that.

I: Oh I see, you mean you would check to
       see if your answer was the same as hers?

P$_2$:   They would show the real answer, the right
       answer, on the board. If you check over
       somebody else's work and you'd give, we
       did that last year and we passed over
       some. You take some person's work and
       you check over it to see if you got all
       your work right. You would take your
       own paper and check over.

Terry does not appear to share the values that the
teacher attaches to checking, nor does she seem to
understand the basic procedures for checking. She
has apparently tried repeatedly to arrive at the
'right' answer in the past without success; consequently she has given up on checking as a monitoring strategy. Carol, on the other hand, agrees
that there is some value in checking, but her definition of it is very different from the teacher's;
'checking' to Carol simply means comparing her
answers to the teacher's 'right' answer, or to
other students' answers.
     The teacher's view that the students have
been taught and, therefore, must know how to check
their math work is not validated by the evidence;
however, the teacher's suggestion that her students
expect her to check their work does receive some
support. The teacher appears to under estimate
the difficulties faced by her students when they
are asked to check their math work. Successful
checking (or monitoring) presupposes: (1) that the
student is competent in basic mathematical opera-
tions, such that errors can be detected; and (2)
that knowledge of correction procedures, including
estimation and prediction, are available. These
competencies even when developed by 'learning
disabled' children are often inaccessible, as their
diminished confidence in their stock of knowledge
results in the adoption of the stragegy of 'playing
it safe', exhibited in Terry's abandonment of her

checking procedures, and Carol's delight in using presumably 'right' answers of others. The two students seem to be operating, at least in the maths class, with a general formulaic strategy in learning.

INDIVIDUAL DIFFERENCES AND SCHOOL COMPETENCE

Differences among pupils in academic performance can be understood by referring not only to variations in academic and social-cognitive knowledge as Mehan (1980) suggests, but by considering possible significant effects of differences in metacognitive knowledge. To return to the topic of the monitoring of comprehension, it is conceivable that students who closely monitor their understanding of a mathematical task may select a different and more appropriate problem-solving approach if and when it appears that they are not making progress. On the other hand, students who monitor their performances in a casual manner may miss the clues that indicate they are not on the right track, so that faced with difficulties they cannot precisely define they might be inclined to give up, as Terry did, rather than to persist with the work.

It is conceivable that a student who typically employs a 'close monitoring' strategy for a given set of school problems will be more likely to adopt the generative mode of learning and its associated student role of producer, or co-producer, of knowledge. The corresponding hypothesis is that a student who typically adheres to the 'casual monitoring' strategy for a given set of school problems will adopt the formulaic mode of learning and with it the student role of reproducer of knowledge. The performances of Terry and Carol seem to fit this latter characterisation. However, it is likely that every student will follow a 'close monitoring' strategy for some school problems and a 'casual monitoring' strategy for others. If this is the case the student, if observed for a long enough time period, will likely vacillate from independence of the teacher to dependence on her as a function, among other things, of the subject-matter being taught and the specific context of learning, including the quality of personal relationships in the classroom.

One clear suggestion from the results of part of the clinical assessment of Terry and Carol is that they conferred their own meaning on school experience which did not coincide with what had been proposed by the teacher. This conception of students as shapers and interpreters of experience receives general support from the psychological theory of human action espoused by Von Cranach(1982). From such a theory it is possible to predict that students would inevitably develop alternative conceptions of 'school mathematics', or any other part of the formal and informal curriculum, which would be quite distinct from the 'authorised' versions. What the student's 'alternative conception or framework' may be is,however,problematic, in fact we are very far from having an adequate account of the student's interpretation of school work. However, we have started to develop such an account in studies where the clinical assessment procedure, essentially a refined interview, has been employed. Present evidence suggests that it provides a useful set of practices for the investigation of the student's world of experience. This technique should prove useful to the teacher for assessing student knowledge, interests and values, as well as for validating the content of lessons. Information so gained will inevitably add to our knowledge of students and therefore have significant consequences for teaching and for structuring the curriculum.

REFERENCES

Birdwhistell, R. Kinesics and Context, Philadelphia; University of Pennsylvania Press, 1970.
Brown, A. Metacognitive development and reading. In R.L. Spiro, et al Theoretical issues in reading comprehension. New York: Erlbaum Associates, 1980.
Erickson, E. and Shultz, J. When is a context? Some issues and methods in the analysis of social competence. In J.Green and C. Wallat (Eds.) Ethnography and language in educational settings. Norwood, N.J.: Ablex Publishing, 1981, 147-160.
Flavell, J.H. Metacognition and cognitive monitoring: a new area of cognitive-developmental enquiry. American Psychologist, 1979, 34, 10.
MacWhinney, B. and Osser, H. Verbal planning functions in children's speech. Child Development, 1977, 48, 978-985.
Mehan, H. The competent student. Anthropology and Education Quarterly, 1980, 11, 3, 131-152.
Osser, H. The structure of children's school knowledge Revue de Phonetique Appliquée, 1980, 55-56, 231-242.

Osser, H. 'The child's construction of the social
    order of the classroom' in F. Lowenthal and
    J. Cordier (eds), Language and Language
    Acquisition, New York: Plenum Press, 1982.
Rowntree, D. Assessing Students, London: Harper
    and Row, 1977.
Von Cranach, M. The psychological study of goal-
    directed action: basic issues. In M. Von
    Cranach and R Harré (Eds.), The Analysis
    of Action. Cambridge: Cambridge University
    Press, 1982, 35-73.
Walker, R. and Adelman, C. A Guide to Classroom
    Observation. London: Methuen, 1975.

Chapter Twelve

SWEEPING PORRIDGE UPHILL: ATTEMPTS TO CHANGE
TEACHERS' METHODS AND ATTITUDES

Anthony Cassidy

THE PROBLEM

A major obstacle to genuine curriculum change is the
resistance of teachers. As well as the normal human
distrust of the new, the particular conditions in
which teachers work, and the attitudes commonly
found among them, make the process of change in
education extremely slow. This resistance is not
so pronounced when the changes involve simple matters
of curriculum content: most teachers accept with
philosophical endurance the whims of examination
boards and universities, which determine that a new
area of knowledge or body of information is to be
added to next year's syllabus. But changes in
teaching methods, the organisation of relationships
between teacher and pupil, or shifts in perception
of educational priorities, are all likely to have
a long and difficult birth, which few of them
survive.
    The result is that the real curriculum - that
is, the sum total of experiences undergone by
pupils - has actually changed a lot less in the
last forty years than many people suppose. There
was some ironic amusement to be gained from the
massive HMI report Aspects of Secondary Education
(1979)[1] which surveyed more than 25,000 lessons in
350 secondary schools. At a time when the popular
press, and populist politicians, were calling for
an end to trendy experiments and radical changes of
method, and for a return to authority, control,
and direct instruction in the basics, the HMI report
soberly concluded that the vast majority of pupils
were still lectured at in traditional fashion by
uninspiring teachers, concerned too much with
covering the examination syllabus and keeping the

class quiet. There may have been many changes in educational theory, and a vast amount of research and theorising about the nature of the learning process, but the actual practice of teaching in secondary schools plodded on in time-honoured fashion.

This chapter attempts to examine how and why teachers resist change, so that, for example, an insistence on facts as opposed to skills, silence rather than discussion, passive acceptance instead of self-initiated learning, and writing in place of doing are all still the staple curriculum diet in my experience, for most secondary pupils, in spite of all the historical, social and educational pressures to reverse these priorities. This discussion of teacher resistance to change will be based not on any broad, theoretical perspective, but on an account of several initiatives undertaken by the author in Comprehensive Schools while working as a teacher, each attempting to focus attention on a particular problem, heighten awareness of the factors involved, and implement change in classroom methodology across the curriculum. In short, it will consist of a series of linked anecdotes. But while these experiences are specific to particular institutions, I believe that they raise implications for anyone involved in strategies for encouraging professional development, school-wide self-evaluation, and a co-operative sharing of ideas and experiences between teachers.

PHASE ONE: SOME INITIAL MISTAKES

In the Spring of 1980, while working as a teacher of English in a suburban Comprehensive School, I was invited to take on responsibility for encouraging and developing more effective methods for teaching across the whole curriculum. This new post was created by the Headmaster in response to the HMI report mentioned above and in particular to its recommendations in Chapter 6 on the need for a healthy 'language climate' in schools. To some extent this was a development and extension of the familiar proposals of the Bullock Report[2] on the need for awareness of the role of language across the curriculum, but in view of the confusion and apprehension this formula had provoked among teachers, we settled on the more flexible soubriquet of 'Communication in Learning'. The aim was to develop teacher awareness of the processes involved in such areas as the role of writing in

the classroom, question and answer techniques,
pupil talk, group discussion, reading for research,
and so on, in the hope of assimilating many of the
recent theoretical and research insights into
teachers' practice, as well as generating cross-
curricular co-operation and mutual understanding.
The Headmaster's vision in recognising the need
for this sort of staff development was not, as
it turned out, invariably shared by his staff.

My first move was to form a Working Party
with representatives from as many subject departments as possible, and with a cross-section of
seniority from Heads of Faculty to Scale One teachers,
in order to ensure the widest possible dissemination
and influence of ideas. A list was drawn up in con-
sultation with the Headmaster, who then personally
invited each nominee to join. This apparently
simple first step was to give rise to problems,
which are discussed below. Our first group contained
teachers of English, Physics, Chemistry, History,
Geography, Mathematics, Craft, Home Economics, French,
and Religious Education.

After a meeting to clarify general aims and
methods, I decided, fairly arbitrarily, on pupils'
written work as our first area of inquiry. I had a
suspicion that pupils spent an excessive amount of
time writing, and that much of the writing was in
itself fairly pointless. This suspicion was confirmed
by our first piece of research as a group, which
showed that an 'average' pupil, during the Fourth
and Fifth years leading up to external examinations,
wrote nearly 320,000 words, plus about 400 pages of
mathematical exercises. An average paperback book
is about 60-70,000 words. Moreover, about two-thirds
of this staggering volume of written work, excluding
the Maths, consisted of either notes which were
dictated, copied, or lifted from a single text-book,
or mechanical exercises testing recall or simple
comprehension . If we are aiming to develop relevant
intellectual social and personal skills, this situation seemed to me to be highly unsatisfactory.

In discussion with the Working Party, however,
it became apparent that my expectation that they
would share my dismay was somewhat naive. Many of
the teachers seemed to feel that the value of such
written work was self-evident, since it kept the
children quiet, made sure the syllabus was 'covered',
and provided the pupils with the necessary factual
information, which was seen as the teacher's primary
responsibility. The statistics summarised above
simply proved that the pupils were 'working well'.

To counteract this complacency, I began furnishing items for group discussion drawn from recent research and theoretical publications. These stressed such matters as the usefulness of purposeful writing having a clearly defined audience and communicative function; the use which can be made of personal discursive styles as opposed to impersonal 'transactional' writing, so ubiquitous in schools yet so alien to most children; the need for practice in neglected areas such as re-drafting, synthesising and interpreting data instead of single-source copying, and the marshalling of opinion and argument.[3]

These outside sources met with polite, momentary interest, or simple rejection as irrelevant to the day-to-day exigencies of 'getting through the syllabus' or 'making sure they've got all the notes'. I supplemented them with some minor work of my own, which involved getting students in an English lesson to write up an experiment from their previous Chemistry class, using spontaneous personal language instead of the passive-voice, 'objective' style usually demanded of them. A subsequent questionnaire to the pupils concerned had revealed that they found the expressive style much more useful for generating understanding of the processes involved. The Science staff on the Working Party were unimpressed. Recording the facts was paramount; it was even maintained that 'understanding' was a superfluous luxury, at least until the Sixth Form.

The original purpose of the Working Party was that it should provide a source of new ideas and approaches, which would then rapidly filter through to the rest of the staff. It was obviously foundering. The reasons for this failure, however, proved interesting and instructive in themselves. Commitment to its aims, and even comprehension of them, was obviously mixed. When originally constituting the group, I had opted for nomination rather than a simple request for volunteers. This procedure was designed to prevent a situation where the group could be characterised as some sort of lunatic fringe, and safely ignored. In the event, this choice was a mistake. The more senior members of staff present were, generally speaking, the most entrenched and unreflective in their views, and the most skilled at avoiding any commitment to practical change.

A second mistake on my part was the attempt to feed theory into practice. Most teachers view educational research and theory with suspicion, indifference, or what they see as a robust contempt. 'It's all very well for these professors/

educationalists/researchers to pontificate; they
don't have to take 2c on a Friday afternoon/get 5g
through O level Geography/keep Billy Sproston in his
desk'.

Thirdly, it began to emerge that many Comprehensive teachers operate on a very simple, unexamined
philosophy and psychology of education, derived from
their commitment to academic subject disciplines,
which assumes that their job consists of shifting
factual information from their end of the room to
the end occupied by the pupils. Any view of teaching
and learning which presupposes attention to skills,
processes, concepts and attitudes, is likely to be
met with defensive suspicion, or evasive lip-service.

This fundamental problem in perception became
much more apparent when the discussions of the Working
Party were published to the whole staff as a discussio
document, which they in turn discussed in groups and
in plenary session at a Staff Meeting. Reactions
ranged from mild, detached interest, through baffle-
ment, cynicism, to outright hostility. A Chemistry
teacher reacted in outrage to the discussion on
expressive versus transactional writing: 'its my job
to train scientists; I have to stamp out any personal opinions or reactions'. My inquiry as to what
proportion of his Comprehensive pupils went on to
become practising Scientists met with a snort of
indignation. Many teachers echoed a Historian's
view that 'it was all a lot of extra work dreamed up
by (the author) to justify his Scale point'.

In general terms as an exercise in encouraging
changes in method and approach, the experiment had
obviously been a failure. However, there were
isolated pockets of genuine interest among committed
individuals, and I had learned several strategic
lessons.

PHASE TWO: VOLUNTEERS AND PRACTICAL INTERVENTION

For the next phase I decided to use a voluntary
group, and to intervene directly in classroom
practice, avoiding theoretical discussion. An
announcement was made at a Staff Meeting that a
group was to be set up which would look at the
possibilities of learning through talking, rather
than through writing. The initial response was
encouraging: about a dozen teachers of English,
History, Social Studies, Art, RE, French, Maths,
Geography, Craft, and Home Economics. Sadly, no
members of the original co-opted group attended,
which seemed to be a judgement on our original

lack of perspicacity in their selection.

At the first two meetings we discussed, in a general way, the usefulness of pupil talk, particularly in small groups, and the organisational problems involved. I then raised the idea of a 'Talk Day' on which every teacher in the school would organise their lessons exclusively or primarily around small group activities involving discussion. The group responded with a mixture of enthusiasm for the idea, and a realistic sense that the proposition, and the view of learning it implied, ran counter to the prevailing orthodoxy of the school. Fortunately, the support of the Headmaster could be relied upon, but from many staff we anticipated misunderstanding or resistance. So in subsequent meetings we evolved a strategy which would, we hoped, overcome these.

A handout was issued to staff, setting out briefly the benefits of carefully structured small group discussion, in terms of a) the immediate learning situation - assimilation of new information and concepts, relating them productively to existing knowledge, understanding processes and their application etc, b) the long-term development of the child-increased confidence and articulacy, ability to explore one's own ideas and modify them in response to others, practice in co-operative problem solving, awareness of how attitudes and values affect rational judgements etc, c) increased motivation when the pupil is actively involved in the learning process rather than a passive recipient of 'knowledge'.

An in-service training session was organised involving the staff taking the role of pupils, in a one-hour session after school. The total of 84 staff was divided into twelve groups, taking care that each group contained a representative from each faculty, and where possible from different subjects. The school computer was used to sort out the groupings. Twelve separate 'group talk' lessons were laid on, each in a separate room, and each led by a member of the Learning Through Talking group. We deliberately chose activities which could be applied in many different subject areas - simulation games, group problem solving, role play, consensus decision-making etc. We also tried to choose a variety of activities in terms of the types of learning taking place. After 25 minutes the groups rotated, so that every teacher experienced two talk lessons.

Faculty meetings were organised for the following week, at which colleagues could give a brief

233

summary of the activities they had experienced,
indicate the types of learning taking place, and
suggest ways in which each particular technique could
be modified to be relevant to their subject. To
assist staff at these meetings, I issued a handout
summarising what had taken place at the in-service
session. This seemed necessary as some staff seemed
unable to perceive what 'learning' had actually
taken place.

On 'Talk Day' itself, each member of staff
was to organise his or her lessons for one day
around small-group talk activities. For maximum
impact I had originally hoped that this could all
take place on the same day, but. after various
objections a week was chosen, and each teacher
chose a day within that week, indicating their
choice on a notice in the Staff Room.

A questionnaire was issued afterwards, asking
basically for a) a brief summary of the lesson
which had worked best, indicating in what ways it
has been successful, and b) a brief summary of
the least successful lesson, with suggested explanations why.

Finally, the next Staff Meeting was a follow-up
discussion.

Throughout this sequence, several difficulties
had to be overcome. Personal defensiveness was an
immediate problem, as teachers felt their private
classroom domain threatened, and was compounded
here in some quarters by the feeling that the Talk
Day plan implied criticism of their habitual teaching
methods, or an assertion of professional superiority
by English teachers. The solution was largely
presentational. The content and tone of announcements
in meetings, printed handouts, and personal lobbying
had continually to emphasise the co-operative,
experimental and constructive nature of the exercise.
To quote from one handout.

> We hope that all colleagues will approach
> this exercise in a positive spirit, and
> regard it not as an imposition, but as a
> lively and challenging opportunity to
> experiment with and evaluate, and hope-
> fully to improve, the quality of learning
> in our classrooms.

Eventually this approach seemed to pay off, and
reflex hostility and suspicion abated.

Misunderstanding of the basic idea was
fairly widespread, and sometimes seemed almost

deliberate. A Physics teacher remarked:

> It's all very well having discussions
> in English and RE, where there are
> <u>opinions</u> to discuss. Science is
> about <u>facts</u>. We can't waste time dis-
> agreeing about established facts.

The assertion that group talk necessarily involved
the sort of value judgement found in RE, or generalised conversation found in English, was a narrow
mis-reading of our basic premise, i.e. the potential
versatility of structured, purposeful discussion.
It became obvious through informal feedback that
many colleagues had an extremely vague and limited
idea of what <u>types of</u> small group activity could
be organised. This lack of imagination led to
outright hostility in some cases. It was to meet
these objections that we organised the in-service
session, described above.

The in-service session helped to clear up
misunderstanding and allay hostility. It also
provided colleagues with plenty of ideas to adapt
for their own lessons, and the general level of
interest became high. However, the fundamental
problem mentioned earlier, where 'learning' is
equated simply with 'memorising factual content',
once again caused difficulties. As one French
teacher remarked dismissively, after the session:

> I've planned the layout of an imaginary
> suburb, and played around with mathematical
> patterns. So what? What have I really
> learned?

To deal with the immediate problem, a sheet was
issued giving a brief summary of the types of
learning which I believed were taking place in
each of the activities.

Another underlying prejudice which began
to appear related to the notion of 'work', e.g.
'Its all very well doing all this talking, but
when are they going to get any <u>work</u> done?' 'Work'
is a word used with extreme frequency in schools,
often acquiring an almost totemic significance, e.g.
'Robert must work harder'.... 'Did 3c do any work
today?'....'We've covered most of this year's
work.....' 'They always work less in the afternoon..'
'He did some work for a change' etc. Unfortunately,
'work' almost always translates as 'written or
practical work done with silent concentration'. It

was obvious, therefore, to certain members of staff,
that if pupils were 'merely talking', they could not
be doing any work.

In an attempt to counteract this attitude,
I suggested, at a meeting, a semantic experiment
in which we all substituted the word 'learn' for
'work' whenever possible. For example, instead of
saying 'Did Sam do any work today', substitute
'Did Sam learn anything today', or instead of
'3C have worked hard this week', substitute '3C
learned a lot this week'. The clear implication
was that a pupil could be 'working very hard' and
learning very little.

Whether this suggestion had any long-term
effect on attitudes is difficult to establish,
but it certainly had considerable initial impact.
We heard no more complaints about talking not being
work.

Inertia was the final barrier. As the week
approached which we had selected for the exercise
a sheet was put on the Staffroom noticeboard, where
staff were supposed to sign up to indicate which day
they had selected to be their 'Talk Day'. In spite
of all the energy which had been put into preparations
by the group, all the interest aroused at the in-
service session, and the verbal agreement of nearly
all staff, by the Thursday preceding Talk Week, only
about a dozen teachers had signed up. A final push
to overcome inertia was obviously needed.

Each morning, the school had a 'bulletin' session
at which all staff were present for announcements
and day-to-day administration. On Friday morning I
announced in ironic tones that the Headmaster had
agreed that anyone not signing up would be timetabled
for the following year to teach exclusively in the
boys' toilets. There was nervous laughter. By lunch-
time there were seventy-eight signatures on the list.
A combination of humour and veiled threat had
obviously worked.

Feedback through the questionnaire was overwhelmingly positive. The vast majority of teachers
found their particular 'Talk Day' experiences highly
enlightening. Many were startled by mature response
from pupils and the productive learning sessions which
resulted. Most stated categorically that the experience would influence their approach in future. The
'Talk Day' experiment had been a success.

Two main principles emerged from all this
activity. Direct intervention in classroom practice,
rather than abstract persuasion, is essential for
instigating change. Secondly, it became apparent

236

that the necessary starting point for genuine
curriculum development is to enlist as many
teachers as possible in looking closely at
existing practice. As a first step, the routinely
familiar must be made strange, so that questioning
of its validity can begin.

PHASE THREE: RESEARCH IN PRACTICE AND PRACTICAL
RESEARCH

Around this time I was involved with the Schools
Council Action Research Project: Teacher-Pupil
Interaction and the Quality of Learning, at one of
the outer network centres at Manchester Polytechnic[4].
A group of teachers and lecturers from different
institutions had been taping lessons, transcribing
them, and meeting to discuss the results.
    The use of lesson transcripts seemed to accord
with the principles just mentioned, so I issued
an invitation, at a Staff meeting, to any colleagues
interested in researching their own classroom interactions through the medium of transcripts. My aim
was to introduce yet another Trojan Horse into the
school, which would provoke yet more discussion,
and hopefully development, of classroom practice.
    The response was modest. The first series of
meetings were attended by myself and teachers of
History, Maths, Art, English, French and RE. My
first act was to provide a transcript of one of my
own lessons; it seemed obvious that I had no right
to request such self-exposure from colleagues without
sticking my own neck out first. This was the first
of many interesting sessions, as each group member
produced a transcript in turn, which was discussed
in detail.
    It is beyond the scope of this chapter to dis-
cuss our findings; a full summary of them can be
found in Action Research in Classrooms and Schools.[5]
Many of our observations involved a radical reappraisal of habitual practices. These often pain-
ful insights were forced upon us by the embarrassing
actuality of the transcripts. Even those observations
which were not particularly original, and could
probably have been culled from reading educational
texts, had been arrived at through studying the
particularities of our own lessons, and therefore
had a psychological and professional impact which no
book could equal.
    The next step was to allow this data to influence
the whole staff. At an Autumn 'in-service' day, the
group presented a talk on our observations, from

transcripts, illustrated by members of the group
reading edited highlights, taking the parts of
teacher and pupils. The dramatic, and particularly
the humorous aspects of this approach were very
useful in overcoming all the usual resistances
and hostilities which one encounters when a large
body of teachers suspect that one is telling them
how they should teach.

Feedback was highly positive, both from
follow-up structured discussion groups, and inform-
ally from a large number of colleagues. Many teachers expressed gratitutde that In-Service Training was
at last addressing itself to the actualities of classroom interaction, instead of yet more theoretical
perspectives. In terms of effecting long-term changes
in practice, the signs were favourable. This approach,
with its combination of empirical research and crafty
showmanship, seemed to have hit the spot.

CONCLUSION: A NEW BEGINNING

Unfortunately, I was not able to confirm this impression, as shortly afterwards I moved to another
school as Senior Teacher. Among my responsibilities
are Staff Development, and Classroom Research. At
present I am working with a group of colleagues on
a breakdown of the curriculum as it is actually
experienced by a sample group of pupils. A week
was chosen at random, and questionnaires issued to
all teachers of one particular second year group,
asking for precise details of what actually took
place in their lessons that week. The group of
children were interviewed each day about their
perceptions of the previous day's lessons. Longer
interviews were transcribed. Heads of Faculty were
asked to summarise their curriculum aims for the
second year. All this data was then synthesised into
a report which gave, for example, the percentages
of pupil time spent on writing of various kinds,
practical work, question and answer, group work,
reading etc. The over-duplication of particular
skill training was thus highlighted, as well as the
total neglect of some important curriculum experiences. The section summarising pupils' recollections
of the week's lessons was particularly sobering.

As yet the data has not been presented to the
staff as a whole. The now familiar responses
will no doubt be forthcoming.

Instigating and encouraging change in teachers'
methods and attitudes can be like sweeping porridge
uphill, through long grass. Large injections of

time, energy, patience and ingenuity are required
to produce even the smallest discernible result.
Once this is accepted, however, and expectations
revised accordingly, the exercise can be rewarding,
and genuine progress can be made. Without the sort
of detailed engagement with the problem of teacher
resistance which I have attempted to describe here,
any change in the curriculum is likely to be
superficial, and more apparent than real.

NOTES

1. _Aspects of Secondary Education_, Her
Majesty's Inspectors, 1979.
2. Bullock Report, _A Language for Life_,
Her Majesty's Stationery Office, 1975.
3. see _Writing and Learning Across the
Curriculum_; Schools Council Project, Ward Locke
Educational 1976; _Language, the Learner and the
School_, D Barnes, J Britton and H Rosen, Penguin,
1969, _From Communication to Curriculum_, D Barnes,
Penguin 1976.
4. Reported in G Payne and E C Cuff (eds)
Talk and More Talk: Studies in Classroom Interaction,
Manchester Polytechnic, 1983.
5. For full discussion of this data see _Action
Research in Classrooms and Schools_, edited by
A Cassidy, E Cuff, D Hustler; George Allen and
Unwin, 1985.

Accounts
11
Adelman, C
96,216,217,218
Adolescence
36
Alienation
132,133
Alternative Curriculum
Strategies(ACS)Project
10,54,61f
Anderson, A
156,165
Anderson, Digby
174, 179,195,196
Anthropological Strangeness
139, 178
Apple, M
131
Arnold, H
163
Ashman, I
3,9,53
Assessment
3,143,175,214-227
Bailey, C
107, 135
Bailey, John
2,9,33
Ball, S
133, 134
Barnes, D
127,130,133,135,200,239
Bennett, N
141,166
Bernstein, B
6,13,114

Bettleheim, B
169
Birdwhistell, R
217
Bissex, G
160,167,170
Blass, R
169
Bridges, D
107,135
Britton, J
239
Brown, A
221
Bullock Report
72,229,239
Burke, C
155,165
Butler, D
160
Button, L
67
Brumbaugh, F
157
Buxton, L
70,76-78,98
Calkins, L
160
Cassidy, A
2,177,228,239
Certificate of
Prevocational Educa-
tion (CPVE)
65
Chanon, G
44

NOTES ON CONTRIBUTORS

Digby Anderson is Director of the Social Affairs
    Unit, London.
Ian Ashman is Development Officer, MSC Programmes,
    London Borough of Lambeth.
John Bailey is Chief Inspector, Bedfordshire.
Tony Cassidy is Senior Teacher at Marple Ridge
    High School, Stockport.
Ted Cuff is Head of the Department of Educational
    Studies, Didsbury School of Education,
    Manchester Polytechnic.
Carol Cummings is Deputy Head of St. Matthews
    C of E Primary School, Stretford, Manchester.
Brian Davies is Professor of Education, Centre for
    Science and Mathematics Education, Chelsea
    College, University of London.
John Evans teaches the Sociology of Education and
    Physical Education in the Department of
    Physical Education, Faculty of Educational
    Studies, University of Southampton.
Nigel Hall is Senior Lecturer in Education, Didsbury
    School of Education, Manchester Polytechnic.
Jack Hogbin is Principal Lecturer in Religious
    Education, Didsbury School of Education,
    Manchester Polytechnic.
Dave Hustler is Principal Lecturer in Education,
    Didsbury School of Education, Manchester
    Polytechnic.
John McIntosh teaches Sociology in De la Salle
    Sixth Form College, Manchester.
Harry Osser is Professor of Education, Queens
    University, Ontario, Canada.
George Payne was Principal Lecturer in Education
    and Head of Sociology, Didsbury School of
    Education, Manchester Polytechnic. He died
    on 23 December 1983.
Elaine Ridge teaches at Nechall Primary School,
    Birmingham.
John Robinson is Head of Department of Social
    Studies at De la Salle Sixth Form College,
    Manchester.